THE TRUTH ABOUT HORSES

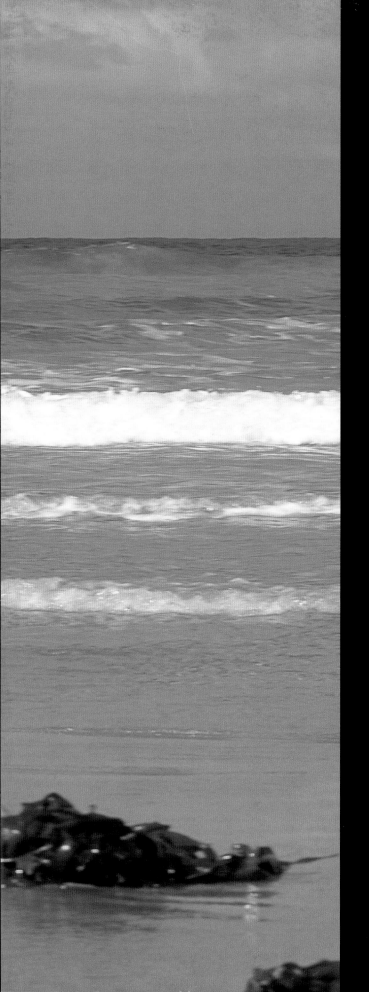

THE TRUTH ABOUT HORSES

A GUIDE TO UNDERSTANDING AND TRAINING YOUR HORSE

Andrew McLean

BARRON'S

A QUARTO BOOK

First edition for the United States, its territories and dependencies, and Canada published in 2003 by Barron's Educational Series, Inc.

All inquiries should be addressed to:
Barron's Educational Series, Inc.
250 Wireless Boulevard
Hauppauge, New York 11788
http://www.barronseduc.com

International Standard Book No. 0-7641-5553-9

Library of Congress Catalog Card No. 2001099143

Conceived, designed, and produced by
Quarto Publishing plc
The Old Brewery
6 Blundell Street
London N7 9BH

QUAR.UYH

Senior project editor *Nadia Naqib*
Senior art editor *Penny Cobb*
Copy editor *Sue Viccars*
Designers *Pete Laws, Karin Skånberg, SheilaVolpe*
Icon artworks *Kuo Kang Chen*
Photographer *Paul Forrester*
Picture researcher *Sandra Assersohn*
Indexer *Pamela Ellis*

Art director *Moira Clinch*
Publisher *Piers Spence*

Manufactured by Universal Graphics Pte Ltd, Singapore

Printed by Midas Printing International Limited, China

9 8 7 6 5 4 3 2 1

CONTENTS

The author, publisher, and copyright holder can accept no liability for injuries sustained as a result of the training methods described in this book. Always take all necessary safety precautions.

INTRODUCTION

King Island lies in the wild Bass Strait that separates mainland Australia from Tasmania. The McLean family arrived there in 1970 as refugees from a business failure and in search of a fresh start. As far as I was concerned, it was the best decision my parents ever made. The island's shores, lagoons, and coastal hills were filled with wildlife: a paradise for a child obsessed with animals. My friends and I spent our time on horseback, galloping bareback around the hills, chasing kangaroos and peacocks, and collecting snakes and birds.

For a community of only 2,000, King Islanders don't lack entertainment—clubs and societies exist to cater to every interest—but horse racing has been a consuming passion since the foundation of the racing club in the early 1900s. When I was growing up each race meeting would finish off with an open affair over 3 furlongs, or 650 yards (600 m). You could ride any breed; saddles were not required, and the only stipulation was that the horse had to be grass fed. I entered one of these races on a Thoroughbred mare borrowed from our neighbors. Sired by a freakishly small stallion, Meadow Jane was the hardest, most uncomfortable horse I ever rode bareback. She had a long back and was not quite 14hh, but she was never beaten on the island's racecourse or along the beach.

My introduction to eventing came about unexpectedly. One summer, a guest instructor came to teach our Pony Club camp, and asked four of us if we would like to go to the State Championship horse trials in Tasmania. Horse trials (or three-day eventing) is like a triathlon for horses, with three phases: dressage, cross-country, and show jumping. Our horses were scarcely trained at all and were practiced in only one gait—the gallop—but we decided to have a go.

My views on horse training were defined by two very different experiences in my eighteenth year. First I saw a quiet and tractable horse transformed into a very tense animal after a traditional breaking in that involved a lot of driving (walking behind the horse with long reins) and sacking out (flailing the horse with a hessian bag, supposedly to quiet it). Then I saw my friend Bill Osborne transform a very nervous horse into one that was calm under saddle. Bill used the Jeffery Method, learned from Maurice Wright, author of the book on the subject. I decided that I was going to start young horses using the same method, in which touch and body contact are pivotal throughout the breaking-in period to prevent the horse from perceiving that it is being chased by its human handler.

On my return to King Island, John Rhodes and Hilary Wiltshire gave me the chance to start their young pacers and stock horses. I broke them in with the lead rope in one hand and the Jeffery Method textbook in the other; by the time I finished my university studies I had started or retrained 50 young horses. I got a job teaching biology and after a year went part-time so that I could spend more time working with young horses. I also pursued my interest in eventing, and gained some success at the state and national level. It was the combination of this competitive experience and my academic study that

Below, left to right

My horse Sam's ancestors swam ashore from a shipwreck of horses bound from Ireland to Australia in the 1800s. My friend Brett Thorn and I were the first to circumnavigate King Island on horseback (180 miles [288 km]) in 1975.

led me to question the basis of conventional horse training. How is it that we train horses without knowing learning theory? Dog trainers and trainers of zoo and circus animals are well versed in this; why not horse trainers? It seemed that most successful horse trainers used aspects of learning theory without being aware of the principles of what they were doing. Perhaps this is why very good trainers are regarded as "gifted" rather than knowledgeable.

I continued to teach while my wife, Manuela, and I established and developed Woodmount Equestrian Centre. We began to employ those aspects of learning theory that we understood, and tried to translate them into training practice. Gradually we gained a reputation for being able to resolve behavior problems in horses.

Around this time I was informed that if I wanted to represent Australia at eventing again I should relocate to the mainland. This dovetailed with my plans to do some postgraduate study in ethology—the science of animal behavior—especially in the area of training psychology, so we left Tasmania for Clonbinane in Central Victoria.

The aim of my research was to find out how training could be improved if it were to incorporate behavioral psychology. It seemed to me that all contemporary training methods implied that horses had human-like abilities to reason, and that this fact alone reduced the chances of success in training.

My Ph.D. supervisors, Associate Professor Rolf Beilharz and Professor Paul Hemsworth, were enthusiastic supporters of my research, and were instrumental in the publication of "Cognitive abilities—the result of selective pressures on food acquisition?" in the journal *Applied Animal Behavior Science*. This exercise opened many doors for me; my background was in animal behavior (a branch of zoology) and I now found myself hurled into the disciplines of cognitive science, most relevant to the study of the mental abilities of horses.

During this time Manuela and I established the Australian Equine Behaviour Centre, where we train and retrain hundreds of horses every year, and coach riders of all ages and skill levels. We give clinics and seminars all over Australia. We have developed a comprehensive system for training young horses based on a blend of ethology and behavioral psychology, which is also effective in rehabilitating horses with all kinds of behavioral problems. It is a simple system, based on establishing (or in the case of retraining, inadvertently re-establishing) consistent, reliable responses from single signals. The common thread in treating all behavior problems is that when the horse becomes free of confusion and consistent in its responses, a calm, soft attentiveness follows.

This book concentrates on those aspects of behavior that impact upon horse training, rather than providing a general understanding of all the senses, behaviors, and instincts of the horse. The reader will come to understand not only how training becomes incorporated into horse behavior, but also why training failures occur.

Andrew McLean

Below, left to right

We shipped our horses to the Pony Club titles in Tasmania, and I then began show jumping competitively. While experiences on King Island taught me "stickability," my jumping position needed some adjustment!

> *"We swallow at one gulp a lie which flatters us, but only drop by drop, a truth which is bitter to us."*
>
> *Diderot*

CHAPTER 1 THE LAST FRONTIER

IMAGINE WHAT MIGHT HAVE HAPPENED IF A FLEET OF AIRCRAFT HAD APPEARED ON EARTH THOUSANDS OF YEARS AGO. THE LOCAL INHABITANTS, ONCE THEY HAD OVERCOME THEIR FEAR, WOULD HAVE FALLEN VICTIM TO THEIR OWN CURIOSITY. AFTER MUCH EXPERIMENTATION AND MANY FAILED ATTEMPTS, SOMEONE, SOMEHOW, WOULD HAVE MADE ONE OF THE PLANES FLY.

How would this individual explain to a culture with no experience with machines how he managed to work this giant metal bird? Was it the pressing of the pedal? The pulling of the stick? Or was it more to do with the subtleties of posture, attitude, or self-belief? The world's first pilot would acquire a godlike status, and much time would be spent speculating over what went on in the minds of the fabulous flying beasts. Their existence would be chronicled in art and story and they would be thought of as not only beautiful but also courageous and spirited. They would be likened to birds because that was what they most closely resembled. No matter how

hard or how diligently the people applied their brain power to solving the many mysteries of the metal birds, their understanding would be limited, not by their mental abilities, but by their restricted mind-set.

The horse came to humanity in much the same way as the aircraft in the above story. Of course, it didn't just arrive—we had been eating horses for eons before eventually someone caught, tamed, and trained one. But the first humans to ride horses must have been revered by all who saw them. Their abilities would have been seen as a gift possessed by very few, and something that set these people apart. It is not surprising that skilled horsemanship has always been greatly admired and viewed as something special. Until the twentieth century nobody had identified the learning mechanisms behind equestrian methodology, and scientists such as Thorndike, Pavlov, Watson, Hull, and Skinner had yet to deliver their extraordinary insights to the world. Even today the frontiers of equitation have not been challenged by science because, in many ways, the horse is still seen in the same light as the jet plane in the story.

No one comes to a discussion of the horse empty-handed: We arrive with the burden of 6,000

> **" We will probably still be riding horses in the next millennium providing our training and management practices are deemed humane and ethical by future generations. "**

years of accumulated knowledge, gratitude, myth, and hearsay. Our two species are permanently and inextricably linked. Over the centuries we have trained horses to perform successfully in many spheres of the human experience, including agriculture, sport, and war. They have lived and died beside us and it is hard to imagine what our lives would be like if their domestication had never occurred. We will probably still be riding horses in the next millennium providing our training and management practices are deemed humane and ethical by future generations.

Folklore and equestrian traditions have led us to believe that the relationship between horses and humans is virtually preordained. We think of this relationship in terms of mutual benefit and define it with words like "trust" and "partnership" that imply an equal motivation toward a common goal. From early childhood we grow up with the notion of the benevolent horse such as Black Beauty. We hear Olympic-standard equestrian competitors ascribe their achievements to the partnership with their horse, the high levels of mutual trust and confidence, and the horse's bravery and willingness. Yet, for every so-called "brave," "determined," and "loyal" horse there is apparently another that is "lazy," "stubborn," or even "bad." For every equine success story there is another of trials and strife, and we accept this because we believe that some horses are less intelligent and less cooperative than others. There is a strong tradition of heroic "cures" of these recalcitrant individuals and even today most saddlery shops stock equipment that is designed for just that purpose.

Above and right
Horses have been used throughout the centuries for agriculture, war, sport, and transport.

Right *To "cure" vices in horses, mankind has invented all sorts of devices. Unfortunately, these methods attend to the symptoms rather than the causes of problems.*

There was a time when I didn't question the role that animals played in our lives. Sheep were there to be shorn, horses to be ridden, cows to be milked. They were just like us, only unable to talk and not quite as smart. They were mostly eager to please, they "understood" punishment and reward, and their lives were governed by the necessity of the jobs they were there to do. After all, these animals knew what was required from them and any deviation from that was simply naughtiness or stupidity. I now know that I was wrong.

Redefining the relationship

Modern science has given us a new perspective from which to view our domestic livestock and companion animals, yet we remain strangely reluctant to question the commonly accepted view of the horse as the willing, courageous, intelligent animal of lore. But the deeper we look into the relationship between horses and humans, the more we become aware of problems that cannot be resolved by the traditional mind-set, or within the framework of mutual partnership. One example is the wastage statistics for the horse industry, which are unacceptably high. The most eminent researchers, Ödberg and Bouisseau, found in a study conducted in 1999 that of 3,000 non-racing horses sent to the slaughterhouse in France between the ages of two and seven years, 66.4 percent were condemned for "inappropriate behavior." The fact that these statistics come from countries with well-established equestrian traditions gives no grounds for believing that the figures would be much different elsewhere.

Below *Racehorses are defined by their "will to win," while warhorses were lauded for their bravery.*

Inevitably, we view the world from our human perspective. We can never really know what it is to be a horse. Our best hope is to be as objective as possible and to balance our emotional attachment to the horse with our tradition of rational inquiry. To do this we need to redefine the way that we think about the horse using the science of behavior. One might wonder why this hasn't been attempted before now. The answer probably has to do with what we want to believe. Myth, history, and popular culture depict the horse–human relationship in ways that do not acknowledge disturbing wastage statistics. After all, existing methods of horse training have always worked to some extent, and in some cases have been highly successful.

As a species we empathize with the horse, and although this is understandable it has contributed to the problems in the horse–human relationship. In projecting our own personality onto the horse we lose sight of the animal as it truly is. Anthropomorphism (the attribution of human form or personality to animals) seems an inescapable part of the husbandry of all domestic animals. In Europe in the Middle Ages pigs were commonly put on trial. Records describe how, in 1457, a sow was hanged for murder but her six piglets, although found guilty of being accessories, were pardoned because their extreme youth made them unlikely to realize the enormity of their crime. As recently as the 1960s a rhinoceros was elected by a large majority to the city council in São Paulo, Brazil. Even today some animal rights activists are campaigning to give chimpanzees full human rights under law.

The assumption of knowledge

These acts of anthropomorphism are only marginally more absurd than some of the assumptions that are made about the horse. One of the most detrimental is the assumption that the horse "knows," and therefore knows the difference between right and wrong, which makes it appropriate to dole out punishment when it is guilty of "wrong" behavior. *The brain of the horse is simply not capable of complex thought*; expecting it to conform to a training system that assumes it *is* capable is not only unrealistic but also unethical. Imagine trying to teach a cat to fly—it doesn't matter how many times it is thrown into the air, it will never fly because it lacks the appropriate physical structures. No matter how many times the horse is punished for its apparent "stupidity" it will never learn to reason because it, too, lacks the necessary physical structures.

Only if we abandon our humanistic model of horse behavior and adopt one based on a more objective view will we be able to celebrate the differences between our species. We will then be able to structure our training systems so that they make the most of the horse's excellent memory and reduce conflicts associated with poor training techniques. The horse's brain has been superbly but exclusively adapted for its life as a grazer—we can ride and drive the horse because we "hijack" the structures that were established for this purpose—and knowledge of the way it works can only help us to train more efficiently and with less stress for the horse.

The end of the "thinking" horse

In 1888, Wilhelm Von Osten set out to prove his theory that animals were able to work out solutions to problems almost as well as humans. Priding himself in his great teaching skills, Von Osten trained a horse in basic arithmetic in front of a blackboard, rewarding correct answers with morsels of carrot. Clever Hans became famous the world over for his counting skills,

Below *When a horse does not carry out its rider's wishes, it is frequently blamed for being "difficult."*

tapping out with his hoof mostly correct answers to basic counting questions. Early investigators reckoned the horse to have the the mathematical ability of a 14-year-old child—he could even do square root calculations! When Von Osten was confronted by his critics, he remained unshaken in his belief that his was a "thinking" horse, and he petitioned the emperor to order a scientific investigation.

Thirteen investigators—including a zoologist, a veterinarian, a circus trainer, and even a politician—were commissioned by the Berlin Psychological Institute, and they could not find the slightest trace of fraud. They ordered a more thorough investigation, and this time it was observed that the horse could not give the right answer if the questioner did not know the solution. Normally Hans would read each card and tap out the answer, but when Von Osten did not know which card the horse was being shown, Hans made mistake after mistake. Further experiments revealed that Clever Hans was responding not to the questions, but to almost imperceptible visual cues in his trainer. In anticipation of the correct answer, Von Osten would inadvertently straighten his posture or subtly change his facial expression, and that was the cue for the horse to stop tapping his hoof. Even a slight raising of the trainer's eyebrows was sufficient cue for the horse to stop. Some believe that the audience behind Von Osten were also guilty of inadvertently providing cues to let the horse know when to stop pawing. In any case, the ruined Von Osten felt Clever Hans had let him down, not realizing that he had unknowingly conditioned the horse to the raising of a brow, and he died a bitter and disillusioned man.

The Clever Hans story stands as a telling testament to the pitfalls of the humanistic interpretation of animal behavior. Although Clever Hans lost his reputation as a thinker, it was nonetheless a stunning demonstration of the effectiveness of training, and it shows how the most amazing associations can be made by conditioning. If Von Osten and those around him had not been so preoccupied with discovering some kind of humanlike intelligence in the horse they would have been able to celebrate Von Osten's accomplishments as a trainer, and would have marveled at the horse's acute sensitivity to physical gestures, instead of being disappointed at its lack of mathematical ability. In order to avoid the mistakes of our ancestors we must understand the horse

Left Von Osten challenged Clever Hans using cards with complex arithmetic. Hans would paw the ground the correct number of times, unless Van Osten himself did not know the question.

> *The Clever Hans story shows how the most amazing associations can be made by conditioning.*

as it truly is, acknowledge the complexity of the relationship between human and horse, and so celebrate the differences between our two species.

The truth about horses

In my experience as a trainer, not only of horses but also of horse trainers, I have discovered that many otherwise rational people feel threatened when confronted by the possibility that scientific objectivity might affect their relationship with their horse. Some believe that the adoption of scientifically proven training practices is somehow cold and unloving. But any knowledge that gives us greater insights into the horse's brain and results in clearer learning outcomes can only improve the relationship between humans and horses.

Our understanding of the horse is by no means complete. New research is being conducted all the time and some of our ideas about horse behavior may change as science proves or refutes them. It is my hope that through this book I will lead you, the reader, to question the way we think about the animals with whom we share our lives, and bring you a little closer to the scientific truth about horses.

> *Hast thou given the horse strength?*
> *Hast thou clothed his neck in thunder?*
> *The glory of his nostrils is terrible.*
> *He paweth in the valley and rejoiceth in his strength.*

The Book of Job

CHAPTER 2 THE HORSE AND MAN

MANY REASONS HAVE BEEN PUT FORWARD TO EXPLAIN WHY THE HORSE WAS DOMESTICATED AROUND 6,000 YEARS AGO. HORSE LOVERS HAVE TENDED TO PREFER ROMANTIC EXPLANATIONS, WHILE ARCHAEOLOGISTS TELL US THAT THE HORSE WAS ORIGINALLY USED BY HUNTER-GATHERERS IN EUROPE AS A SOURCE OF FOOD.

The truth, as writer Stephen Budiansky notes, probably lies in the horse's combination of desirable physical and mental attributes—its speed and sociability and its ability to thrive on poor-quality grass, to learn by trial and error, and to form habits. Were it not for these characteristics the horse would most certainly have joined the long list of animals that humans have tried to domesticate without success. Once the horse was adopted as a vehicle in territorial disputes, however, it became indispensable. Its subsequent impact on society was such that it is not hard to understand why it was worshiped by almost every culture that possessed it. For the Greek soldier-philosopher Xenophon (d.360 B.C.E.) and others who rode in wars, the horse was seen as a mighty warrior and a staunch ally:

In my opinion, the man who neglects husbandry matters neglects himself; for it is plain that in moments of danger the master gives his own life into the keeping of his horse.

The same sentiment is apparent in the story of Bucephalus:

Alexander the Great acquired the horse Bucephalus when the horse was 14 and he himself was only 12. When he alone, out of all of his father's grooms, demonstrated an ability to ride the horse, his father wept with joy and said, "You must go look for a kingdom to match you my son; Macedonia is not big enough for you." Alexander had a great fondness for his horse and rode him in many battles over more than 15 years until finally he was killed in 327 B.C.E. On that day Alexander rode recklessly into the enemy's ranks even though he was "the mark for every spear." Many spears were buried in the horse's neck and flanks and although mortally wounded Bucephalus was able to carry Alexander to safety whereupon he died from a great loss of blood. Alexander founded the city of Bucephalia in honour of his horse and grieved for his friend.

Right *In ancient times, the horse was highly valued as a brave and loyal warrior, qualities that were deemed essential to victory in battle.*

Similar stories are told about the mounts of other famous warrior chiefs throughout history. These archetypal myths take their place in our culture not

Right *The story of Alexander the Great and Bucephalus symbolizes the notions of trust and loyalty between horse and man.*

simply because they are good stories; early writers wrote of fierce, heroic horses that sacrificed their lives for their masters because that reflected the role that the horse played in their society.

As the role of the horse in war was superseded by its growing importance in agriculture, the way it was depicted in art and literature also changed. In Cecilia Dabrowski's short story *A Measure of Oats*, a farmer, Tom Davis, takes his team of three horses to plow a paddock. He has raised and trained them himself and is proud of their "willing strength" and obedience. He marvels how, if urged, a horse will "pull till his great heart breaks and he goes down on his knees, unable to rise again, still believing the possessor of the whip-hand comprehends the limits of his endurance." He considers how "there are times when the beasts of God are better creatures than those who have dominion over them." While plowing the paddock, Tom falls off the seat and lands between the horses and the plow. Although he could easily have been killed he is able to call out "Whoa" to the team, and they stop. He is suddenly aware that he owes his life to their obedience. He marvels:

An apple, a measure of oats, the brief pleasure of a small reward, was all he had to offer in return for his life. He was hurtfully conscious of the inability to communicate his reason for gratitude, acutely aware of the impeachable trust that is given to those with dominion over the beasts of the earth.

Farmers had every reason to be grateful to their horses because their livelihoods (and often their lives)

New Age trainers have had a very positive impact on horses; they emphasize gentle, nonviolent training techniques.

explain the success of their training. These terms are, however, not without their problems, as will later become apparent.

Some trainers allude to a special affinity between women and horses. The internationally known Native American trainer GaWaNi Pony Boy says, "Throughout my life there have been several occasions in which I have found myself in awe of the bond that exists between women and horses." One of the best examples of the New Age approach is the story of Shy Boy. This was a wild mustang that Monty Roberts tamed with his "Join Up" method. The horse was habituated to saddle, bridle, and rider and became a useful mount. After several months Monty decided to test the bond between himself and the horse and he released it back into the herd. It stayed with the herd for one night but returned to him in the morning. Monty explains, "All by himself Shy Boy exhibited his true freedom and chose to come home." This story clearly reinforces the New Age notion of horse training; it illustrates the duality of the bond between horse and owner, and speaks of the innate "goodness" of the horse.

Although it is difficult to overstate the amount of good that has been done by the New Age trainers, it is important to see their contribution to our understanding of the horse in the historical context. Throughout history the horse has been depicted in many different ways, and it is clear that this has more to do with how we *use* the horse than with what the horse really *is*. New Age trainers have developed

Left The closest species to a prehistoric type still in existence today, Przewalski's horse came perilously close to extinction. It has now been re-introduced to its former habitat in Eurasia.

Below In the past, farmers' livelihoods often depended on their horses. The horses' strength meant that they could cultivate large fields and pull heavy loads to market.

depended on them. Steadfastness, reliability, and obedience were qualities to be prized, and celebrated in story and art.

The rise of the New Age trainers

Horses have a variety of uses today, and this is reflected in the way we see them. Horses used for sports are still most often described like horses that were used for war, with the emphasis on their "bravery" and "will to win." But the most significant development in equestrianism since the early 1980s has been the rise of the "New Age" trainers, who have introduced an entirely new vocabulary that includes terms like "respect," "attitude," "partnership," and even "love." This new way of perceiving horses is based in leisure and the niche that the horse fills in our society today—that of companion and friend. New Age trainers have had a very positive impact on horses; they emphasize gentle, nonviolent training techniques and urge riders to understand and empathize with their horses. They use elements of the horse's wild behavior (such as its herd instincts and hierarchical social structure) to

within the context of the "horse-as-companion" relationship, and this context has influenced the way they view, train, and manage horses.

The science of animal behavior

Less than half a century ago, there were just two major areas of inquiry into the behavior of living things: the study of animal behavior (ethology), and the study of human behavior (psychology). Today behavioral science encompasses many areas of research, including neuropsychology, applied ethology, and the latest addition, evolutionary psychology.

During the optimistic decades of the 1950s and 1960s people grew increasingly suspicious of science, with its cold reputation and increased potential for destruction, and many began to look for alternative ways of viewing the world. Dreadful scientific accidents such as the thalidomide tragedy seemed ample justification for rejecting the science that promised much but couldn't provide all the answers. At the same time, however, significant advances were being made in the field of behaviorist psychology.

The most influential behavioral psychologist of all, B. F. Skinner, published an extraordinary paper in the first half of the twentieth century entitled "The Behaviour of Organisms" in which he outlined the principles of "learning theory." This theory is accepted and practiced today by almost all animal trainers—with the exception of horse trainers. Two of Skinner's students trained a number of animal species to do a variety of tricks, but found that his principles could not be applied to all behaviors in all animals. For example, pigs are good at pushing levers with their snouts but not so good at doing it with their feet. Frequently their animals would revert to

"species-specific" behaviors: pigs would root around in the ground with their snouts; chickens scratch with their feet; raccoons would lick themselves. Skinner's students published a paper aptly entitled "The Misbehavior of Organisms."

This was a disaster for the science of behavior and the search for the exact mechanisms of learning. Skinner's behaviorist model was replaced by cognitive psychology, which maintained that behavior is too complex to understand in purely mechanistic terms. But in recent years the pendulum has slowly swung back. Behaviorist theory provides concrete prescriptions for behavior modification in humans and animals. Behaviorist programs are regularly employed to provide cures for learning disabilities and delinquency in humans, while practically all animal trainers use behaviorist theory. Models of behavior exist that demonstrate how animals make choices in a multichoice setting, not by any conscious "understanding," but by showing that there is a mathematical predictability about choice-making that can be explained in terms of previous reward and practice.

There is still a major polarization in ideas about animal behavior that has resulted from the differences between ethology and psychology. One of the most respected cognitive scientists, Sara Shettleworth, published a review of animal cognition, or mental

processes, in 2000. She pointed out that the science of ethology arose mostly in Europe within the discipline of zoology, with its strong emphasis on evolution. Psychology, on the other hand, largely evolved in North America without the influence of the evolutionary perspective. Zoologists typically look for meaning in animal behavior in terms of adaptations to environments. Psychologists look primarily for causal principles of behavior.

My early background in behavioral science placed me solidly in the zoology camp. But when I embarked on my Ph.D. I began to be influenced by the psychological viewpoint. Today the sciences of ethology and psychology are merging closer than ever before, and this book reflects this integration because training involves dealing with instinctive patterns of behavior as well as learning mechanisms.

Many of the New Age horse psychologists and horse-whisperers latched on to the zoological viewpoint for the majority of their insights into the equine mind, but filled in the gaps with erroneous assumptions of humanlike mental abilities. These gaps would have been better filled by psychology.

Many contemporary methods emphasize the predator-prey phenomenon in human-horse interactions, but then describe the latter in terms of the horse accepting and regarding the human with respect and as a leader. They emphasize the importance of factors such as eye contact between humans and horses, and the belief that eye contact is seen by the horse as a threatening gesture. However, a recent study published in *Applied Animal Behavior Science* suggested that eye contact with humans makes no significant difference to horse behavior. Other questionable concepts, such as the suggestion that trainers "negotiate deals" with their subjects in much the same way that predators and prey "negotiate deals" in the wild, are illogical and based on a human-centered view of equine behavior.

The slow evolution of the behavioral sciences, and the lack of knowledge about these among trainers of horses, has hindered progress. There are much simpler, more plausible explanations for the dynamics

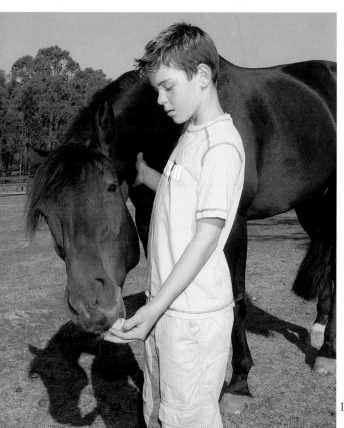

Left At some point almost every child dreams of spending time with a horse.

> ❝ *The New Age notion of horse training speaks of the innate goodness of the horse.* ❞

Above *Sound training at an early stage of a horse's development can be highly effective. U.S. veterinarian Robert Miller (not shown) has written extensively on the enormous capacity of foals to learn precociously.*

of social behaviors in horses than the implication of human reasoning abilities. New Age philosophies have certainly provided solutions to some problems that traditional equitation methods could not. But they have not provided all the answers because their methods do not embrace modern learning theory. Real progress in animal cognition can only occur when there is some integration of *all* the behavioral sciences.

The theory of learning

Horse training is a long way from being considered part of the realm of science. Much research has been done on the processes of learning, yet this has yet to be incorporated into horse training in any meaningful way. The majority of equestrian texts written in English, even those written since 1960 (post-Skinner), fail to incorporate any aspects of learning theory at all; most go only so far as mentioning using kindness in all interactions.

Learning theory provides clear-cut answers for why certain outcomes occur in training, yet some trainers continue to attribute some aspects of training to extrasensory perception or even telepathy. Other texts show a total disregard for scientific knowledge about the capabilities of the horse's brain. The following quote, from the journal of the reputable *Equine Behaviour Study Circle*, is fairly typical of certain trends in current equestrian literature. This journal regularly publishes accurate scientific content about aspects of behavior such as windsucking and

weaving, but when it comes to describing the horse's mental capabilities, it is sometimes surprisingly off the mark:

Depressed, timid, or bullied horses can have their self-respect restored when groomed by the handler in front of other horses. One farm places such horses in the barn aisle way, in full view of the other horses, for 15 or 30 minutes of concentrated, loving attention. The other horses interpret such attention as the right of an important animal.

Horse trainers worldwide use a fairly consistent set of physical cues, called "aids," to train horses: The reins of the bridle give the cue for stopping and turning the horse, and the legs of the rider make the horse go forward. Associated cues such as changes in weight, voice, and seat are also often used, usually after the horse has learned the rein and leg aids. (We will examine these in much greater detail in Chapter Four.) This has led many riders to believe that domestic horses are somehow born with these cues preprogrammed in place. The truth is that the horse has simply grasped the correct response during trial-and-error learning. The failure of horses to comply with the aids is often seen as a moral failing on the part of the horse, not a failure of the training system.

The current preoccupation with rider mechanics and the lack of emphasis on learning also illustrates the absence of real scientific understanding in horse training. While riders must be able to sit in independent balance in order to apply the aids

Right *A sound knowledge of training principles and psychology is vital to the safety and well-being of all riders, especially young ones.*

consistently, the effectiveness of associated cues such as the seat can be explained by conditioning. The body of the rider cannot "mold" the body of the horse until the rider has an extremely high degree of control over the horse's speed and direction, yet there are whole books devoted to ways of sitting and rider posture without reference to training.

Horse training is not a magical process; it is a systematic science. Horse trainers of previous centuries are often referred to by modern trainers as "Old Masters," whose work is not to be questioned. While it is extremely interesting to see how in some of these early texts the workings and effect of learning theory could already be seen, these talented horse trainers learned their trade by "second nature," without knowing the theoretical framework upon which all animal training rests. In 1560 Thomas Blundeville, a well-respected trainer, suggested this method of training the "reluctant" horse to go forward:

Let a footman stand behind you with a lively cat tied at the one end of a long pole with her belly upward, so that she may have her mouth and claws at liberty. When your horse stops or goes backwards, let him thrust the cat between his thighs so that she may scratch and bite him, sometimes on the thighs, sometimes on the rump and often on the testicles. A similar correction may also be given with a puppy or some other loud crying and biting beast being tied to the crupper, so that he may hang down under the horse's tail.

This quote may illustrate some knowledge of how a horse might learn to go forward, but it also reveals the pitfalls of blind acceptance of the Great Masters' work.

Learning theory explains how learning occurs and gives clear guidelines for effective training; aspects of it have been used, knowingly or otherwise, by horse trainers for thousands of years. But trainers who worked pre-Skinner never had access to the whole body of theory; they were building jigsaw puzzles with half the pieces missing. At various times throughout history trainers have had all the pieces at their disposal, but never all at one time. Some of their insights have been forgotten or ignored by succeeding generations of trainers. For example, Baucher, a nineteenth-century trainer, recognized the importance of not allowing trained signals to clash. His maxim of "Main sans jambes, jambes sans main" (hand without legs, legs without hand) seems perfectly logical: in other

words, don't press the brake and the gas pedals at the same time. Tom Roberts, a well-known twentieth-century Australian horse trainer, maintained the same principles.

Yet much of modern dressage training defies this principle by, for example, maintaining the horse's outline with an excessive degree of rein contact. This leads to a tight and uncomfortable neck and many problems in the mouth of the horse. The French have another saying about this: "The wire needn't be tightened for the power to flow."

I will discuss more about the effects of rein contact in Chapter 7. For now we will move from what we think we know about the horse to what we actually do know: let us examine the horse's true nature as revealed by the objective inquiries of science.

Above The wastage rate in the sport of dressage could be reduced significantly if riders adopted the principles of training psychology.

" Horse training is not a magical process; it is a systematic science. "

CHAPTER

3

THE CENTAUR

LURKING IN THE DEEPEST CANYONS OF OUR PSYCHE IS THE NEED TO DISCOVER THAT WE ARE NOT ALONE ON THIS PLANET. WE SEARCH SPACE FOR ALIENS, AND PROBE THE MINDS OF ANIMALS IN THE HOPE OF FINDING ECHOES OF OUR OWN HUMANITY. THE CLOSER TO OUR HEART AN ANIMAL LIES, THE MORE WE WISH TO FIND A SIMILAR INTELLIGENCE. BUT WE MUST PUT THIS DESIRE ASIDE AND LOOK OBJECTIVELY AT WHAT WE KNOW ABOUT THE BRAIN OF THE HORSE.

Understanding and comprehending are abilities that we take for granted. They involve ideas. Can animals have ideas? Can animals lead complex lives without being able to understand and comprehend? The mechanisms of learning in animals have evolved to allow for very complicated and clever behavior, but how can we discover what animals such as horses are mentally capable of?

We can investigate the results of experimental tests that demonstrate the presence or absence of higher mental faculties, such as reasoning. We can look to evolutionary psychology and ask ourselves: What sort of mental abilities should we expect to find in the horse? What would it need to evolve? And we can

examine the anatomy of the horse's brain. Brain parts and functions are fairly standard in mammals. By noting the presence and degree of development of various brain parts, we can deduce quite accurately what the horse is capable of. Combining these three approaches should give the clearest possible picture of the horse's mental abilities.

Before we begin our examination, we must first be clear on our scientific ground rules. Over the centuries philosophers and scientists have come up with logical ways of determining what is likely to be right from what is likely to be wrong in our thinking and assumptions. Two of these concern us here.

The first is the Law of Parsimony, also known as Occam's Razor, after William of Occam, the

fourteenth-century English philosopher. When it comes to determining the nature of something (such as how intelligent horses are), Occam implores us to accept the simplest possible explanation, until any more complex one can be demonstrated beyond doubt. This theory cautions us against overestimating the capabilities of any given entity (such as the horse).

The second is the Null Hypothesis. This says that we must begin any inquiry with no assumptions.

Above Although increasingly pampered over the course of the last century, horses constitute a tough and sturdy species of animal; one that is well adapted to harsh weather conditions.

Right Humans have little difficulty developing strong emotional attachments to horses. However, this may act to the detriment of the horse if people assume that the horse has a human-like intelligence.

The best-known null hypothesis in our culture is the phrase "innocent until proven guilty." In order to amass a clear picture of the mental abilities of the horse, we should assume nothing, then build on it.

Daniel Dennett, an authority in the area of animal mentality, cautions that assuming, without proof, that animals possess higher mental abilities "is to ignore the Null Hypothesis in an unacceptable way." Perhaps this has been the problem with understanding horses. Few people have set out to determine their mental abilities scientifically because we are afraid to discover that they are anything other than the courageous, loving, and intelligent creatures we have grown up with. Our own emotional attachments act to the detriment of the horse; overestimating its abilities leads to inappropriate training regimes and inadequate management strategies. In assuming that the horse has a humanlike (but lesser) intelligence we risk missing some of the amazing mental abilities it does possess.

No properly conducted scientific test has ever been able to demonstrate any reasoning ability or capability of insight in the horse. All the seemingly clever acts that horses do on a regular basis—such as the pony that, Houdini-like, can open any gate—can be explained by conditioning, not reasoning. It is probably true that if horses could reason, we would not be able to ride them. We must therefore assume that horses do not "think" in the way that we do. We will never know what mental life is like for a horse, but it is safe to say that it bears little resemblance to that of a human.

Experimental evidence

Research indicates the following four criteria as evidence of some higher mental faculties, such as basic reasoning abilities, in animals:

- the ability to imitate *new* motor behavior exhibited by another animal
- the ability to solve *new* problems on the first attempt
- the ability to learn to take shortcuts in mazes, also known as detour learning
- the ability to form concepts

Like most other grazing animals, horses are not adept at any of the above. Published investigations indicate that horses are unable to learn *new* behavior

by observing another horse performing that behavior. For example, although horses are normally very motivated by food, hungry horses do not learn to press levers to obtain hidden food by observing other horses doing it. My own experiments show that horses are unable to reduce their fear of scary places by watching other horses go there.

I am specifically referring here to the learning of new behavior by observation. Most mammals are capable of copying some of the behaviors that are already hard-wired in their repertoires: This is known as social facilitation or contagious behavior, and is similar to the motivation that makes me yawn when I see another person yawning. I haven't learned to yawn by watching someone else do it; the response is simply facilitated by the sight of another doing so. Social facilitation in horses includes horses becoming nervous when they see others doing so, lying down and getting up when others do so, grazing when and where others do, and following the herd—the instinct that allows migration and group cohesiveness. Learning by observation is only evidence of reasoning when the learned behavior is a novel act.

Research also shows that horses are not good at solving novel problems. In what are known as discrimination reversal tests, horses are presented with a choice of two feed buckets, one of which always contains food, while the other contains nothing. The horse has to learn to return to the bucket where it first found the food until its location is switched, after which it has to try the new one, find the food, and return there until the food is switched again, and so on. Some animals, such as chimps, quickly learn the correct approach, but horses are much slower to grasp the rule. Locating grass and herbs requires no problem-solving strategies, so horses have never needed to evolve the higher mental abilities that we take for granted.

The horse also fares badly in maze-learning experiments, where it has to remember how it got to a specific goal placed at the end of a multichoice raceway. Many anecdotal accounts from life confirm this. Professor Waring of Southern Illinois University described how a group of wild horses died of dehydration because they could not work out how to navigate around a straight stretch of fence that had been placed across the path they used to get to their water hole. The journal *Equine Behaviour* related how one group of horses wished to reach another in a neighboring field from which they were separated by a fence; despite the fact that the gate at one end of the fence was open, the horses just stood there whinnying to each other, desperate to make contact, and oblivious to the open gate nearby. Yet these horses had been led through the gate in the past. When eventually one pony did bolt through the gate, the others were unable to follow its example.

When horses learn to do such things by trial and error they are generally able to solve the problem again on a future occasion. But experimental evidence strongly suggests that they cannot "see" the solution without prior practice. The clever things that horses have been known to do, such as open gate latches, are not the result of reasoning, but of trial-and-error learning. What makes us different from horses is that you and I can do this trial and error in our heads.

The evidence of evolution

When Charles Darwin published *On the Origin of Species by Natural Selection* in 1859, his book created both intense scientific interest and public outrage. Darwin's theories have since come to be recognized as some of the most important ever published, and they are fundamental to almost every facet of biology.

Briefly, natural selection is a process of gradual change that species undergo through thousands of generations in order to best fit their environment. Certain individuals within species may vary slightly in a way that gives them an advantage over their contemporaries. Such plants and animals are more likely to survive and therefore pass their variation on to their offspring. Thus, the individuals that best fit their environment survive to breed, and over thousands of years the characteristics of a population change. This is evolution.

Evolution has a streamlining effect on the mental and physical characteristics of a species, discarding unnecessary traits and developing those that are efficient. In the course of evolution (over thousands of generations) the behavior and mental abilities of species continually adjust in response to the challenges they face in their environment.

One of the most significant challenges facing animals is obtaining food, and the evolution of a species is very much driven by the development of characteristics that enable it to do this effectively. The selection pressure required to evolve neural (brain) tissue has to be very strong: The brain is ten times more expensive to run—in terms of the energy it requires—than any other tissue, and shows a definite tendency to regress over the generations if not utilized.

Animals are as insightful as their environments require them to be. For a horse, the finding and obtaining of food requires very little insight. As Budiansky points out, grass, unlike mice, does not hide and cannot run away. The horse's brain is about 3½ inches (9 cm) long by 2⅓ inches (6 cm) wide, and a large proportion of it is devoted to solving the massive engineering problem of propelling 1,000 pounds (450 kg) across the ground at 40 miles (64 km) per hour. Large brains require high-energy diets to run them and the horse, of all the ungulates, has evolved to graze on the poorest of grasses. A nutrient-deficient diet of this sort simply could not support a larger, more human type of brain. Instead the horse's brain has phenomenal memory storage, being able to generalize stimuli (a facility we hijack to the full during training), the ability to learn rapidly through association, and the capacity to make choices between multiple stimuli based on previous reward. Scientists call this "transitive responding," and models of how it works have been shown to be complex—but not to involve reasoning abilities.

According to Darwin, for a characteristic to have developed within a species it must have conferred some survival value on the individual, and therefore an ability to breed more numerously. What is often described as survival of the "fittest" is more accurately summarized as survival of the "best fitting." Evolution is not a race to develop the biggest, strongest, smartest individuals; it is a process that hones species for their environmental niches. Would the development of higher mental abilities have allowed individual horses to produce more foals? The answer is a resounding no. In fact, the ability to reason might actually have a negative value for a species like the horse.

The evidence of anatomy

The horse's brain is perfectly adapted for its life as a social grazer. Some of the advantages of habitual behavior over higher mental processes are:

- repetitive behavior patterns or habits allow for immediate reactions, important for a prey species such as the horse
- habits are stable in expression and are changed only by the shaping effects of conditioning

- habits require less time for learning, an important attribute for animals whose young have to be able to gallop from danger soon after birth
- habits are less costly (in terms of food and energy) than generating insightful, reasoning processes

Most human higher mental processes occur in the parts of the brain known as the right neocortex and the prefrontal cortex. The neocortex is the external section of the brain and is responsible for learning and correlating multiple sensory outputs. Humans, cetaceans (whales and dolphins), and the great apes have extensive surface wrinkling of the neocortex. This increases the surface area and therefore the size of the brain, and allows the development of higher mental abilities. The neocortex in other animals is much smaller, relatively smooth, and is dedicated to other tasks relating to survival such as physical sensitivity and locomotion. Budiansky points out that in horses the neocortex has evolved to allow a greater sensitivity of the lips and mouth, vital in a discriminatory grazer. On the evidence of brain anatomy, however, it is unlikely that the horse is capable of higher mental abilities.

Reasoning in humans evolved to allow greater opportunism, with the result that our ancestors spread across the globe and outwitted animals many times more powerful than themselves. Reasoning was sponsored by our primate ancestry and the planning abilities that accompany manipulative appendages such as grasping hands. This gave rise to the culture and awesome potential of tools and fire. Language further accelerated development of higher mental capabilities, allowing the development of what cognitive scientists refer to as "semantic memory"— the flexible memory of ideas.

Because humans are proud of their reasoning abilities, horse lovers seem determined to prove that horses are capable of reasoning. But reasoning isn't universally useful. Reasoning abilities are responsible for psychotic disorders in humans and are associated with the worst aspects of hatred, revenge, and malice. Reasoning also interferes with memory storage, because our ability to recall memories at will and out of context exposes them to the risk of corruption. Equine memory, on the other hand, is practically photographic, even after many years of storage. Animals such as horses possess amazing abilities because their minds are more associative than reasoning.

> *Evolution is not a race to develop the biggest, strongest, smartest individuals; it is a process that hones species for their environmental niches.*

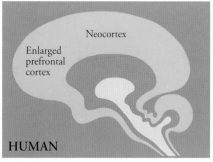
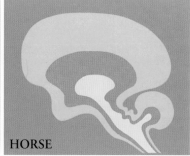

HUMAN   HORSE

Language and the horse

Thought and imagination are inextricably linked to language. Could a species without language think? Certainly not in the way that humans do. Language is a purely human trait, requiring types of brain wiring that other species do not possess.

While some New Age horse psychologists insist that horses have language, the truth is they do not. Animals communicate with each other using a range of sounds, but these sounds "mean" very little; it is what they "achieve" that is important. Whinnies produced by horses are generated in the same ancient parts of the brain that in humans produce crying and laughing. These vocalizations are the same in all humans across the world, just as whinnying in horses is "understood" by horses across the world. Human language, however, is symbolic, learned and generated in specialized areas of our brains that are not present in any other species.

Understanding language is very different from being able to demonstrate certain behaviors in response to verbal cues. Verbal cues are not language; language has structure, form, and categories. Verbal cues are single words or simple phrases that are attached to behaviors via training and repetition. Every few years animal researchers claim to have trained a horse (or chimpanzee, or rat, or pigeon) to "understand" language but in effect what they have done is train a number of reliable verbal cues that elicit reliable responses, a fine example of training, but no demonstration of a species' linguistic abilities.

Above The brain consists of three main parts. The human brain is significantly different from the brains of most other mammals in that it has an enlarged neocortical region— the part involved in higher mental abilities.

Most people who believe that horses "think" like humans cite some of their more complex behaviors as evidence. But this shouldn't fool us into assuming more mental ability than is really there. All animal species are born with a set of hard-wired instincts that allow them to interact successfully with their environment from birth, and these can produce all kinds of complex behaviors. Some of these, such as the bee's, with its innately structured society and its multistory nests, are quite amazing. Yet few would go on to claim that the bee possesses a complex brain and a high level of intelligence. Here again the distinction must be made between intelligent behavior and complex behavior; while the former may be evidence of higher mental abilities, the latter most certainly is not.

During my Ph.D. I wanted to look at the memory recall ability of the horse. In one of my

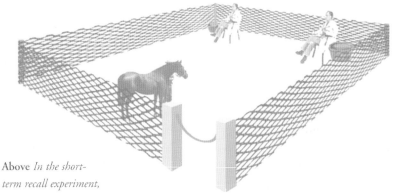

Above In the short-term recall experiment, each horse was released either immediately or 10 seconds after food was poured into the feed bin by the person sitting beside it.

experiments, horses were given two goal choices, two buckets into which feed could be placed. The subject horses were held facing the midline of the two goals but able to see both, and feed was placed, using random schedules, in one of the two buckets. The horse was able to see the food being placed in the bucket. If the horses were released as the food was placed in the buckets they were able to choose the correct goal 75 percent of the time. When delivery of food and release were separated by ten seconds the success rate diminished to 50 percent, or no better than random.

The lack of recall ability is not the same as memory of an episode or procedure. Because the choice is between two similar and previously rewarded responses, this experiment required the horse to remember the last food delivery only, among many previous responses to both goals. This requires

a particular aspect of memory that the horse does not possess, and never needed to possess in its evolution. It added further to my conviction that horse trainers must make rewards immediate and connected to the correct behavior, and should not expect the horse to be able to recall the act that is rewarded, after the event. The same is true for punishment—delayed punishment cannot possibly work. We should not load the horse with our expectations that it "knows" right from wrong, or that it "understands" its training in any way. We are training reactions or responses in the horse, not comprehension.

Horse instincts

As we have seen, horses (and all other animals, including humans) are born with the potential for certain behaviors "hard-wired" in their brains. The term creates a mental picture of the brain (essentially an accurate one) as a giant circuit board with a few switches and microprocessors thrown in. There are literally trillions of possible circuit pathways in the brain, which means that the potential for different behavioral reactions to environmental stimuli is enormous. A favored pathway that becomes "well trodden" through repeated practice becomes a habit. In addition, certain instinctive drives are indelibly etched on the horse's brain: feeding, flight response, fighting, and reproduction. The final expression of these instinctive behaviors is altered by experience, otherwise known as conditioning or learning. Learning is the creation of new pathways in the brain.

When two or more drives compete in the animal's brain the one with the greatest survival value will predominate: extreme fear, for example, will prevail over mild hunger. An animal responds to stimuli in order to reduce whichever instinctive drive has the most survival value at the time. The animal is hungry so it seeks food; when alone it seeks other members of its species, or substitutes; if it feels pain or pressure it seeks to remove the cause.

The flight response

The horse's instinct to run away from danger is called the flight response, and it includes a mosaic of behaviors ranging from mild tension to bucking. The more the flight response is practiced, the more established the neural pathway governing its expression becomes in relation to the stimulus that

Left *Researchers have found that immobilizing a horse's legs and then swinging a bag toward its head has a dramatic calming effect on the horse.*

caused it. The flight response has a high coefficient of reinforcement or "reward"; it takes very few repetitions to consolidate it as a habit. Horse trainers often lament that bad behaviors seem to be learned much faster than good behaviors. The flight response (and associated behaviors such as bolting, bucking, and shying) can be difficult to eradicate once established due to its high reinforcement value. The more the flight response is practiced, the more it begins to appear in connection with other behaviors.

While all the instinctive drives are important in understanding horses, the flight response has the most impact on training. Training inevitably involves raising alertness levels as the horse's behavior is modified, and this sometimes escalates to greater levels of tension and flight response. In contemporary training systems, the tendency is usually to "push him through it," in other words, to allow the expression of the flight response in the hope that the horse might "get over it" and "see that there's no need for it." The outcome, however, tends to be the opposite: The flight response becomes a regular feature of the horse's behavior because of the practice it has had at expressing it.

But because the flight response is expressed by the running of the horse's feet, simply immobilizing or slowing the feet through thorough training of the "stop" (and slowing) responses in hand and under saddle will disengage the association. The horse is literally unable to maintain the fear response if its legs are immobile, slowing, or going backward. This has huge ramifications for training and retraining problem horses.

Animal behaviorist Temple Grandin describes the wheat box, a device that stifles the flight response in wild horses. The horse is placed in a large box, which is then filled with wheat to the horse's neck, thus rendering it completely immobile. Researchers discovered that the box had a dramatic calming effect on the horse that was being restrained. Similar techniques have been used by horse trainers for centuries. Karen Pryor explains in her book *Don't Shoot the Dog* how police horses were trained by tying their legs together while they were lying down before bombarding them with the sorts of stimuli they might encounter in the streets. Blackfoot American Indians used to mount their horses for the first time in deep water or on marshy, swampy ground, which would stop the horse from moving its legs (and soften falls!). In India, the mahouts begin the training of wild juvenile elephants by immobilizing their legs with chains. Harsh horse trainers these days still hobble and truss horses' feet and then "throw" them so they lie on their side. Some even stand on the prostrate animal, believing that this gains them the horse's respect. These practices are not only barbaric, they are quite unnecessary—there are far more ethical ways to gain complete control of the horse's legs.

The extent to which the flight response is expressed varies widely in domestic horses. Draft and packhorse breeds have been selectively bred for a reduced expression, whereas animals bred for racing and galloping show a far stronger tendency. To train horses successfully we should group together all the problem behaviors that involve expressions of the flight response. Milder tension levels produce the following behaviors:

Below *Over the course of their long association with horses, the Blackfoot Indians learned that mounting their horses in swampy ground diminished the horses' flight response.*

- raising of the head and neck carriage
- hollow contracted back
- tail swishing
- wider eyes
- more open nostrils
- shortening and quickening of the steps
- tail overly raised or clamped against the rump

If these conditions persist for longer periods of time or become chronic, then erratic hard-wired behaviors may begin to appear, all of which would, in the wild, have been effective anti-predator maneuvers. These include:

- shying (rapid sideways movements of the forelegs)
- bolting (stampeding or galloping off where the flight response results in the horse largely "switching off" to conditioned responses, including trained controlling responses)
- bucking (leaping, twisting movements with the head between the legs where the hindquarters are kicked up rapidly)
- rearing (where the horse "stands" on its hindlegs)

Trainers must take care not to allow the flight response to become entrenched, and this has interesting implications for practitioners of training techniques that involve chasing the horse in any way. The work of psychologist Joseph Le Doux suggested that allowing the horse to express the flight response in the presence of its human handler should be avoided at the risk of creating permanent fear- and flight-response-related behaviors. As the flight response usually manifests itself in running away, any *quickening* movement should be slowed; the trainer should be able to immediately slow or stop the horse's legs at any time. Training techniques such as round pen work, lungeing, and long reining can—if not very carefully applied—all lead to the horse expressing the flight response. Their long-term benefit, especially if practiced by an amateur or inexperienced trainer, is therefore questionable.

The hierarchy

Horses are social climbers. Living in a group provides security but leads to competition over limited resources such as food and mating partners. Social behaviors limit the amount of fighting within the group, and aggression is usually thwarted by mechanisms of threat and display. The drive to be dominant over other horses propels the horse to test its place in the group from time to time. Disputes over food and sex increase in frequency in the spring when sugar levels in grass rise. Horses have a "sweet tooth," which drives them to seek out the sweetest grasses in early spring and leads them to become robust and restless, and to "test" the social hierarchy.

The use of dominance and submission theories to train the horse is problematic. Initially it seems acceptable to apply these to the position of an animal within a hierarchy, and also to the "attitude" that is assumed to accompany the pecking order. But on closer inspection the theory founders. There is little doubt that animals interpret the position of each member of the group and behave accordingly. But the assumption that an animal's every interaction with humans is related to some aspect of dominance is unfounded. The notion of dominance has led to the generally accepted belief that horses need to "know their place," and to be shown "who is boss." Most systems of training horses throughout the world rely on this belief, which unfortunately often leads to welfare problems for the horse. If a horse "walks all over" its handler, that is, it barges on his/her space, the problem is not one of attitude or lack of respect— it is simply because the horse does not lead straight. The horse's crookedness may be further rewarded by the side-stepping behavior of the handler. However, it is cured not by an "attitude" change on the part of the horse, but by retraining leading straightness.

Flight distance

The closer you approach a wild animal, the greater its tendency to flee. Whatever maneuver the animal performs that increases distance between it and a potential aggressor will be reinforced and therefore repeated under the same conditions. When dealing not only with nervous horses but quiet ones too, care must be taken not to allow the horse to increase the distance between itself and its handler, or behave in a way that results in the handler stepping away. Safety

because the horse is more averse to the flowerpot than to the driving forward aids of the rider. I have often seen very good trainers explain the problem as one of leadership, and yet as soon as they increase the forward pressures (squeeze harder with the legs, tap with the whip) the horse takes a step toward the object, and eventually goes there. That is how the horse learns to go forward in the first place in its early years. The aversive pressures provided by the rider work, not because the pressures demonstrate to the horse that the rider is a strong leader, *but because when the horse steps forward the pressures are removed.* It is common knowledge in eventing that when a skilled rider rides a strange horse for the first time over a jumping course, the horse goes better for him than it does for its usual, less skilled rider, because of the skilled rider's more appropriate use of signals and pressures.

must always be borne in mind, but there are simple ways to prevent avoidance maneuvers escalating into dangerous or difficult behavior. When a horse kicks at the farrier or veterinarian, he should not step back (increase the distance), but step forward and lay a hand on the horse's shoulders (decrease the distance). Horses that panic at the clippers are retrained not by their removal, but by laying them on a less sensitive part of the anatomy, such as the shoulders.

The herd instinct

This refers to the horse's natural tendency to form family groups, and to move about its home range in an ordered group. The herd instinct can be useful in training young horses to go through water or toward places they would normally be averse to. The instinctive tendency to follow is greatest when the horse that follows is almost touching the rump of the one in the lead; the further back the following horse falls, the less its tendency to follow. Many cross-country trainers train young horses to jump fences by following an older, more experienced horse.

The herd instinct can have negative implications for training when horses—especially young, or confused and insecure horses showing conflict behaviors—become "herd bound" and exhibit separation anxiety. This is accompanied by escalating flight response, but is ameliorated by consistent training that follows the principles of learning theory.

Many modern trainers mistakenly believe that the horse under saddle and in hand regards the rider or handler as the "leader of the herd." They claim that the horse that refuses to go near the scary flowerpot at the side of the dressage arena has no respect for the human as a strong leader. This is ridiculous. The real reason is

An honest appreciation

We have seen that the most likely reason horses do the things they do is because they have been rewarded for such behavior in the past. Thus words used to describe behavior that implies reasoning abilities in horses are completely inappropriate. When we watch a horse galloping around a cross-country course and assume that the horse jumps these difficult obstacles because it "trusts" its rider, we are implying that it knows the dangers but chooses to overlook them. Yet in order to negotiate such obstacles successfully the horse has had to learn by jumping smaller ones first. It complies because it has undergone very clear training and has formed consistent habits, and this is why the best riders and trainers regularly produce reliable horses. This is also why some horse/rider

words "cowardly" and "rebellious" imply emotional and intellectual abilities that the horse simply does not possess. Using words that imply emotion or intent is the first step down a slippery slope that leads to believing it to be true. In changing the way we think about the horse, we must change our vocabulary. It is all but impossible to alter beliefs in a fundamental way if the language of the previous belief structure is still in place.

To conclude, it is clear that the horse has quite remarkable powers of memory as well as strong instincts that have evolved for its survival. Measuring and comparing intelligence in animals is fraught with difficulties, and all animals are to a degree intelligent with respect to their own evolved lifestyle. What is certain, however, is that equine mental abilities are only remotely similar to our own, and the acceptance of this is critical to the welfare of domestic horses. We should not load them with our expectations of understanding in training.

The horse is neither a willing nor an unwilling partner. It is a social animal that seems content to form bonds with humans and to form clear habits, even if these are foreign to its instincts. Real love and respect for the horse can only come from an honest appreciation of what it is. Next we will look at how it learns.

Left Horses are naturally curious about unfamiliar things. The foal (above) has not yet learned to shy away from dogs. Horses do not naturally shy away from poles either. Shying (below) is a learned response.

combinations consistently fail, no matter how much the rider loves the horse. We will be better trainers when we see that our job is to *train* the horse to do the things we desire. That involves setting up a clear, consistent reward system. And this in turn must involve thoroughly training the signals and pressures that are an inevitable part of sitting astride an animal with a set of reins in your hands, or standing beside it holding the lead rope.

Similarly, the concepts of "partnership" and "cooperation" must be reevaluated in the light of the emphasis placed upon them by both traditional and New Age trainers. These relationships imply that the horse is somehow responsible for certain aspects of its behavior in training, that it is a willing participant in the training process, whereas in reality the horse is the blameless component in horse-human interactions. *We should see every disobedience as a failure of our timing and reinforcements, not as a failure of the horse.*

Many descriptions are applied to horses: loyal, eager, big-hearted, sneaky, sly, conniving, stubborn, sulky, determined, proud, rebellious, impetuous, cowardly, malicious, impatient, crazy, naughty. Such language is regularly found in mainstream equestrian literature over the past 50 years, and comes with its own baggage. It is impossible to call a horse "impatient" without implying intent. Similarly, the

Below What appears to be a proof of trust between horse and rider is more accurately explained through the correct application of learning theory.

> *Teaching, it is often said, is an art, but we have increasing reason to hope that it may eventually become a science.*

B.F. Skinner 1951

CHAPTER 4
HOW HORSES LEARN

FOALS ARE BORN WITH ABILITIES THAT MAKE THEM APPEAR QUITE ADVANCED COMPARED TO MANY OTHER NEWBORN ANIMALS. IN SCIENTIFIC TERMS THEY ARE DESCRIBED AS "PRECOCIOUS NEONATES." SOON AFTER BIRTH, THEY STAGGER TO THEIR FEET AND BEGIN TO TOTTER ON SHAKY LEGS THAT MOVE BY INSTINCT. THEY LEARN TO STAY ON THEIR FEET THE HARD WAY, THROUGH TRIAL AND ERROR, AND THE CLEAR PRESCRIPTIONS OF SUCCESS AND FAILURE.

They face another early challenge in finding a supply of milk; this again is an instinctive drive that is honed by the reward of suckling. Day after day these drives are shaped by experience through learning. During early training, as a weanling and later in foundation training (breaking in), trainers hijack the various hard-wired mobility responses in the horse to use them for their own ends.

Horses, like other trained animals, only learn behaviors that are already present in the wiring of their brain circuitry. In a sense the horse is born with a ready-made pattern for every behavior it will ever need, such as walk, trot, canter, startle, flying change, and buck. What trainers do is "shape" the expression of these behaviors and train the cues that elicit them.

To learn something means to acquire a new behavior or to modify an existing one. For a human,

memory of stimulus/response relationships, which it will retain, even after many years.

Everyone who knows horses is conscious of their incredible memory. If the bucket outside the stable door is in a different position today from yesterday, the horse may startle at the change. The slightest change on the track—even a fresh line in the sand of the riding arena—and the horse will be aware of it. This acute sensitivity to changes in the environment and the tendency to startle or shy away from them is a product of the horse's evolution. In the wild, spotting the extra lump beside the rocks on the horizon could spell the difference between being alive tomorrow or on the menu of a hungry predator.

Natural selection vs. selective breeding

Domestic horse breeds show a wide variation in the extent to which individuals tend to notice or startle at novel things (this can also be a symptom of confusion or conflict behavior: see p. 39). This is a result of selective breeding by humans, together with the absence of environmental maintenance of the original responses: In the wild, those animals that showed *too little* suspicion of new objects would be eliminated through predation, while those that showed *too much* suspicion would be too fearful and would graze inefficiently. Natural selection would have kept these two extremes within fairly narrow limits.

Selective breeding has enabled us to promote these variable traits, which are to some extent desirable in domestic horses. "Brave" horses that are unafraid of their surroundings and new experiences tend to be easier to train for the cross-country phase of eventing competitions because they have no fear of flapping flags, large crowds, or complex and novel water obstacles. Similarly, "chicken-hearted" horses that are slightly suspicious tend to make better show jumpers because they are more sensitive and tend to be more careful with their legs. Show-jumping horses are often seen wearing earmuffs because they are sometimes a little oversensitive to aural as well as visual stimuli.

It would be naïve to think that wary horses are simply born that way. A horse may be genetically predisposed to behave in one way or another, but the rest is all about learning. Nervous adult horses can be

Above *Horses' gaits are hard-wired into their brain. These include the tendency to "lead" with the inside foreleg during turns in the canter and the ability to accomplish "flying changes" of the leading leg.*
Right *Selective horse breeding for jumping has been a preoccupation for performance horse breeders since the advent of jumping events.*

learning includes acquiring knowledge. This knowledge may never result in any behavioral change, but can remain in our psyches for ages, having no impact on our lives. For an animal such as a horse, however, learning involves the establishment of stimulus/response relationships, where a stimulus from the environment causes a behavioral response. The horse, like most mammals, has a restricted ability to deal with information, yet it also has an awesome

trained to be easily spooked. If the horse is allowed to practice shying away from, or refusing to go somewhere, it may easily develop a habit of aversion. The horse may tend to shy away faster with each repetition, and this can rapidly evolve into spinning away and then rearing away. By this stage the horse has incorporated some fast footwork into its aversive behaviors; this is the flight response, which reinforces the response to the initial stimulus. The horse may now transfer the aversive response to new and random situations; it has learned that running away is a good way of avoiding control by the rider.

Habituation

Trainers of young horses should habituate them, or get them used to, new situations by conditioning the youngsters to respond to the "stop" and "go" signals thoroughly and consistently (see p. 41). This conditioning involves two separate types of learning:

- **Operant conditioning:** This describes training the horse to respond consistently to signals provided by the human, in hand or under saddle, through reinforcement (relief/reward).

- **Classical conditioning:** This involves transferring these learned signals to more subtle versions of the same signal or to entirely new cues altogether.

There are not many scientific terms involved in horse training, but everyone working with horses needs to learn these terms thoroughly, in order to understand the training process.

Above and left A horse's fear of places, or of certain aural or visual stimuli, can be enhanced or reduced depending on experience. Here the rider corrects the horse's action of turning away and trains it to go forward with the use of leg pressures. The horse learns that the rider's leg pressures are more aversive than the small bridge.

Habituation is the simplest form of equine learning. Nothing happens to reinforce a particular behavior either positively or negatively: The horse just "becomes used to" something. Imagine you were to visit a friend who lived near an airport: at first you would probably find the noise of the aircraft distracting. But if you remained in the house for a period of weeks it would become less and less noticeable: this is habituation. For sensitive animals such as horses, the capacity to desensitize to various stimuli (such as the rustling of leaves in the wind) is very important. Habituation in horses has evolved naturally from living in the wild, where animals that reacted repeatedly to every meaningless sight and sound would expend energy needlessly and would, in evolutionary terms, be less efficient and therefore less successful, with fewer offspring.

Horses habituate to many different pressures during training: the pressure of the girth, saddle, the

bit in their mouth, the bridle, blanket, and wraps on their legs. Horses also habituate to the presence of a rider on their back, and to the zone limits of the rider's body and limb movements. This is why even a horse with predictable habits can startle if the rider carries or waves an object outside his or her normal zone. A rider wearing a rustling raincoat or a large hat for the first time can also concern the horse until it habituates to the new experience. The horse does not accept the rider by fuzzy notions of trust, but through the clear mechanisms of habituation.

In order to avoid confusion and conflict, it is essential that the horse remains sensitive to the lightest cues of the handler, driver, or rider. The horse's ability to habituate to stimuli is well developed, so there is great potential for mistakes in training should it habituate to these cues. This must be avoided at all costs. Timing of the signal in relation to the response is critical, and poor timing—removing a signal before the required response is received, for example, or maintaining a signal when the horse has already offered the correct response—is highly detrimental to the horse's development under training.

The application and timing of the aids is largely what differentiates successful trainers from unsuccessful ones. Less successful trainers have a tendency to habituate horses to their signals. Although some horses have a natural tendency to respond energetically to the "go forward" signals, the final expression of the forward reaction is a result of training. Horses labeled "lazy," "stubborn," or "heavy" in the mouth have actually habituated to the leg and rein signals through blurry timing of signals.

Learned helplessness

If an animal experiences pain—for example from severe bits being applied with relentless pressure, or from constant spurring—and finds that no response results in relief, it may gradually habituate to the pain. This phenomenon is known as "learned helplessness." Horses with what is known as a "hard mouth" (an impaired response to cues from the reins) or "dead sides" (an impaired response to cues from the rider's

> *Dressage stallions seem to be particularly susceptible to fatality from what is colloquially termed 'stress colic.'*

Above and right *Even if a horse withdraws its nose but not its feet on sniffing a new object, it must be made to step forward by the trainer.*

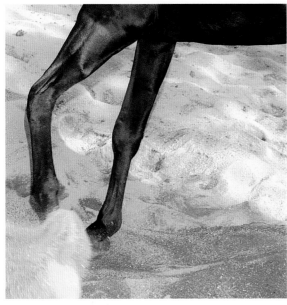

Scientists Maier, Seligman, and Solomon showed certain similarities between the symptoms of learned helplessness in animals and those of depression in humans. These included:

- unwillingness to try out different behaviors in response to pressure
- difficulty in learning that behaviors have outcomes
- lowered levels of aggression
- loss of appetite; physiological and immunological changes

Left and above
Learned helplessness can become manifest in signs of conflict such as pawing and weaving.

legs) may exhibit varying degrees of learned helplessness. Performance horses are often prone to develop this: the corners of their mouths are rubbed raw or split from the pressure of the bit, or they have hairless or cut patches of skin on their sides from the spur. Learned helplessness comes at a high cost in terms of the horse's well-being and may result in chronic conflict and gastric disorders leading to colic, which can be fatal. Dressage stallions seem to be particularly susceptible to fatality from what is colloquially termed "stress colic." Horses that have developed learned helplessness may show other signs of conflict, such as pawing, fence-walking, excessive tension, and even self-mutilation. Any degree of learned helplessness must be avoided in training.

Flooding

The rate at which horses habituate to stimuli varies widely from individual to individual, and from breed to breed. In some cases it can be accelerated by "flooding," or exposing the animal to extreme doses of the stimulus. Flooding is also used to tackle certain phobias in humans—people with a fear of snakes are sometimes helped when forced to confront them in the hands of a trainer—but our complex psyche and imagination confounds the success of this technique. In horses, however, it works well, and it is especially effective if applied while the horse is immobile, as in the example of the wheat-box experiments (p. 29). If you shake a plastic bag at a horse that is loose in a yard, it will run away. Eventually, after many, many

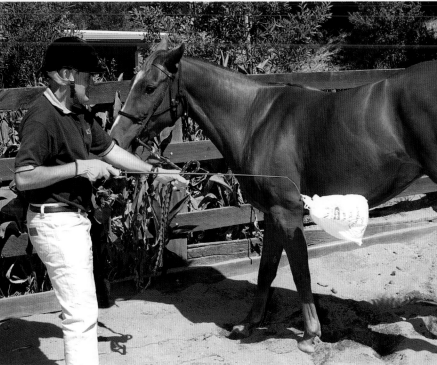

> *Behavior practiced is behavior repeated.*

Above left to right
Desensitizing a horse to stimuli is about disallowing its legs to show the flight response. Here, a plastic bag is repeatedly rubbed on a horse and then swished (on the end of a whip) around it. The horse steps back and forth until it learns to perform the movements in reaction to very light signals.

repetitions, it may habituate to the plastic bag (although its future training may be forever compromised by the amount of flight response it has expressed in the process). But if the horse is made to stand immobile and exposed more gradually to the bag it will habituate with less stress. In horse training this is preferable (and certainly more ethical) than flooding.

Operant conditioning

The most important form of training is known as operant conditioning, also known as trial-and-error learning. The horse learns that when it behaves in a particular way, reward or relief follows, and so it learns to offer the rewarded behaviors.

When motivated by hunger, the horse might learn that if it whinnies or paws the ground, reward in the form of food will follow. It might also learn through trial and error to remove a lid from a feed bucket and obtain food that way. In another scenario, the horse might experience temporary discomfort through pressure on its body. It might discover that a particular maneuver of the body results in the "reward" of removal of the pressure. Subsequently it will offer that maneuver whenever the same pressure is applied. Horses are naturally highly evolved for this:

Any bodily maneuver attempted by the horse during a predatory assault that resulted in the predator losing grip would be used again.

So operant conditioning typically involves two different motivations—food and freedom—resulting from the animal's need to reduce the drive to eat and its drive to be free of discomfort. These embody the two divisions of operant conditioning:

- **Positive reinforcement**: involves the *addition* of something (such as food) to the animal to lower its motivational drive.
- **Negative reinforcement**: involves the *subtraction* of something (such as the removal of pressure) to lower its motivational drive.

Positive reinforcement
Many animal trainers focus only on training via positive reinforcement because their subjects perform at a distance from them. Animals such as dolphins, seals, bears, and dogs, to a large extent, are most often trained in this way. In positive reinforcement, the errors made by the animal are ignored by the trainer. If an animal takes fright during training, the trainer waits until the animal chooses to return to the experimental situation.

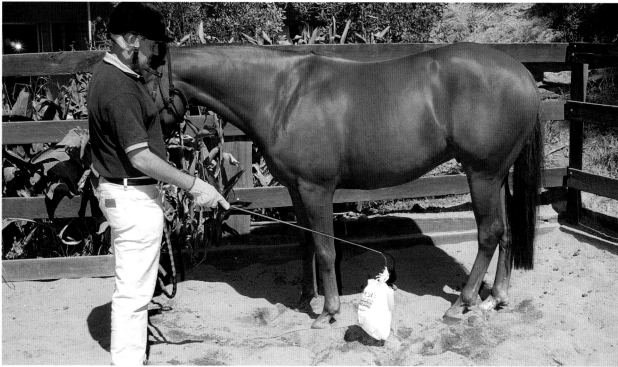

Negative reinforcement

Horse, camel, and working elephant trainers almost universally use negative reinforcement because they work in close proximity with their subjects and can easily administer the pressure cues. Negative reinforcement allows responses (such as stop or go) to be enforced, and signals trained this way have power rather than merely influence.

Under saddle, horses learn to stop when the rider closes the hands on both reins. The rein pressure is released as soon as the horse gives the correct response of slowing or stopping. The horse learns to stop through the reward of the removal of the pressure in its mouth. Similarly, the horse learns to go forward when the rider squeezes or nudges with both legs and then removes the pressure when the horse begins to go forward. The horse also learns to turn through the removal of the pressure of the single rein, and to step sideways with its hindquarters from the pressure and removal of a single leg. Horses rapidly learn to perform these maneuvers in reaction to *very light pressures*: They perceive the initial increase of pressure of either rein or leg and then learn to avoid the stronger pressure. Eventually these responses transform into repetitive behavior patterns, or habits.

Negative reinforcement is used during an incorrect behavior and is discontinued when the

> *Correct use of negative reinforcement results in pressures shrinking rapidly to very light versions of the original pressures.*

targeted behavior begins to emerge. For example, in the early training of the forward response, the trainer applies leg pressure to the horse's sides and releases the pressure when the horse gives a correct or near-correct response of forward motion. Negative reinforcement is based on the following five principles:

- Only the targeted behavior results in the release of pressure.
- The first pressure that the trainer applies is light, because this will later transform into the signal.
- The pressure should be increased consistently; any fluctuation constitutes a reduction in pressure and thus reinforces the wrong behavior. Pressure is increased until the targeted response emerges.
- If intermittent pressures are used (nudging of the rider's legs or tapping of a long whip), there should be no pauses greater than one second so that the horse does not perceive the pause as reinforcing.
- At the onset of the targeted response the pressure

should immediately be discontinued so that the horse recognizes and associates the targeted behavior with the reward.

Negative reinforcement is a process that allows the trainer to delete unwanted behaviors and elicit desirable ones. Applied correctly, it has a number of advantages over positive reinforcement:

1 *Even at higher levels of training the basic responses should be assessed and reinforced. Here the horse is in walk and is about to stop.*

- It allows the trainer to ensure that the response always follows the stimulus. In positive reinforcement, conflict can arise from the severing of stimulus from response, for example, during times of food satiation when the horse may not be "interested."
- Behaviors are usually placed under stimulus control at the onset of training. In positive reinforcement the animal is allowed to practice the behavior randomly before it is placed under stimulus control.
- Because random movements can be corrected and deleted the horse is able to learn consistent stimulus/response relationships rapidly, thus avoiding the conflict associated with escalating random movements, such as flight response.
- The use of bridle and reins allows the horse to learn without practicing errors, such as bolting. This is an important safety consideration.
- The light signal is very quick to initiate. In foundation training, the horse learns to stop from the light rein signal in very few repetitions.

When negative reinforcement is used correctly, minimal physical pressure is required; it is more a matter of irritating the horse to motivate it to give a response. Any pressures, even during retraining, should quickly be reduced to light signals. The pressures

2 *Then stronger pressure is used for the next step if the horse hesitates to stop.*

3 The pressure is released at the onset of the stop.

4 With the "go" response, the rider increases the leg pressure and the horse walks on.

provided by the reins can be reduced through reinforcement to barely perceptible cues. These light cues can be further reinforced to produce subtle variations in the amount of "go" and "stop," rather like the controls on a car. In other words, there is a large degree of "volume control." This is essential for performance horses that require rapid adjustments in speed and direction.

All the cues that we train the horse to respond to in the early phases of training, both in hand and under saddle, should be applied using negative reinforcement. If these are applied thoroughly and consistently, behavior problems can be avoided. Most behavior problems tend to arise in training because of incompleteness or damage to responses trained by negative reinforcement. Unfortunately what tends to happen is that other cues or signals are employed far too quickly to elicit responses; these are generally those described as classical conditioning (see p. 47). For example, initially trained by negative reinforcement from the lead-rope pressure, the lead response cue may be left dormant and half-trained if the horse learns to "follow" the handler. When the horse inadvertently offers incorrect behaviors, such as

5 The rider removes the pressure and the horse continues to walk.

sideways steps, the handler is powerless to correct the problem as the lead response is insufficiently trained. Retraining behavior problems is therefore largely a matter of reinstalling faulty pressure-release responses.

To the horse, operant conditioning can be summed up as: "If it works, do it again." One of the most important rules of training is that behaviors that

usually causes the rider to release contact with the rein. Horses that rear or buck are viewed as naughty or vicious, when these actions are most likely the result of confusion about the rein or leg signals. Alternatively they may be repeating behaviors that have been reinforced inadvertently; in other words, they have been trained to rear and buck from the signals that are

Left and below Here's a dangerous way to lead horses. The long rein and the rider's distance from the horse have allowed it to practice random movements; swerving and shying are common results.

are reinforced will be repeated. For the horse one of the most motivating forms of reinforcement is freedom: freedom from pressure, effort, confinement (physical and visual), and solitude. Food is also reinforcing, but freedom from pressure is the tool that trainers tap into most often. Horses that learn to perform incorrect behaviors—such as bucking and rearing—are usually driven to trial these by conflict, but learn to repeat them via negative reinforcement because these actions almost always remove at least one pressure or control measure. Bucking can remove the rider completely (highly reinforcing!) and rearing

> *One of the most important rules of training is that behaviors that reinforced will be repeated.*

> *Only one aspect of each behavior is shaped at any one time.*

meant to produce "go" or "stop." Retraining reinstalls these basic responses and removes the conflict that initiated them in the first place.

Training-related conflict is often caused by a lack of predictability in the horse's environment. Effective training systems are based on predictable outcomes: The animal is always able to remove the pressure from its body (or obtain the reward) through its newly acquired learned response. The pressures are predictable in that they always start lightly and increase in strength within a similar time frame, and focus on establishing a consistent response.

Shaping

When correct behaviors have been negatively reinforced they can be "shaped" so that eventually they are performed in the same way each time. *Consistent responses arising from consistent signals is the key to calmness.* In most horse behavior problems, responses from signals are frequently random and are generally undesirable ones. Random behavior tends to escalate, and retraining is simply a matter of reconnecting stimulus to response, just as occurs in foundation training.

Shaping is the process of gradually shifting the baseline of what is acceptable in behavior until the desired behavior is achieved. For example, when the horse is initially trained to step sideways, the rider will apply single leg pressure on the horse's rib cage and reward (with softening of the pressure) any sideways movement. Over time the rider can gradually refine the sideways movements by not softening until a greater and greater degree of correctness is achieved.

Shaping can be thought of as rewarding every good try in the initial training, and then refining. *Only one aspect of each behavior is shaped at any one time.*

Stimulus control

When an animal learns to offer behaviors in response to cues, animal trainers say that the behavior is under "stimulus control." For example, all dogs (wild and domestic) sit down; it is a hard-wired behavior that all dogs perform naturally. Trainers put the behavior under stimulus control so that they can make the dog

sit on command. When the trainer can give a cue that results in the dog sitting almost all the time, the sitting behavior is said to be under stimulus control.

Punishment and reward

Punishment refers to any aversive *consequence* of behavior. In horses it mostly does not work, the only exception being where it is applied within one second of the behavior occurring. The use of delayed punishment is doomed to produce conflict and cause the horse's behavior to deteriorate further. While immediate punishment for biting and kicking may be effective, it does nothing to repair the causes of biting (unresolved stop, mouth contact problems) or kicking

Above *To train the horse to move sideways, the rider applies pressure to the horse with one leg until the horse steps across. The goal is to elicit this response using increasingly lighter signals.*

(unresolved forward response and/or contact problems). Punishment after shying typically results in horses continuing to shy but now shying faster and leaping afterward. The further any punishment occurs from its targeted behavior, the lower its chances of success. One of the reasons that punishment is the least effective form of learning is that it doesn't allow the horse (or dog or child…) to practice the correct behavior. Punishment (if it works at all) tells the animal what *not* to do but it doesn't tell the animal what it *should* have done.

Some believe that any use of the whip constitutes punishment. In correct horse training the whip should never be used to punish the horse. It should be used

Above *Horses naturally groom each other at the site in front of the withers.*

only in a tapping motion that increases in intensity to produce a response, such as greater activity, when the rider's legs or the handler's lead rope fail to do so. It is just another training tool, and if used correctly raises no ethical considerations.

Patting and scratching

Many riders use patting to reward their horses, and most would see this as positive reinforcement. But patting can range from gently tapping the hand on the horse's neck to quite violent slapping that must surely be difficult for the horse to distinguish from

> *The horse does not naturally recognize patting as a reward, or find it calming in any way.*

something punishing, or entirely meaningless. Even at the highest level of competition, it is not unusual to see riders, after a good dressage test or jumping round, pat their horses' necks so forcefully that it seems the action is more of a cathartic experience for the rider than the horse. The horse does not naturally recognize patting as a reward, or find it calming in any way. For it to be so, the horse has to learn it. This involves pairing patting with explicit rewards such as food and, in the early stages, never patting unless the horse is receiving food. From the point of view of learning, patting is not a positive reinforcer, but can be a *secondary* positive reinforcer. Another problem is that patting can become the focus of the reward system instead of a release of pressure.

Similarly, expressions of praise such as "Good boy" are quite meaningless to the horse unless they have been trained as a secondary positive reinforcer. The horse does not learn the "meaning" of particular words; they simply become classically conditioned cues. While a loud, harsh voice is aversive to horses, it does not necessarily follow that a low, quiet one is soothing. By virtue of the horse's associative capabilities, however, it is likely that if a low soothing voice is used only when the horse is relaxed, then this voice will in turn assist in producing relaxation. Nonetheless, if we are to train effectively we should be careful to distinguish what rewards behavior from what actually calms the horse.

In the field, horses often stand neck over neck, mutually grooming. They tend to focus mainly on the withers, raking each other with their teeth. Researchers Feh and de Mazières showed that scratching horses at the base of their withers causes a lowering of heart rate; it relaxes them. The further away from this site horses are groomed, the less relaxing the effect. This implies that the horse possesses a useful relaxation "spot" right in front of the saddle and within arm's reach of the rider.

The release of pressure itself is intrinsically reinforcing. It may be confusing to use secondary positive reinforcers at the same time as negative reinforcement. But as soon as any behavior begins to become consolidated, and is elicited each time from a light version of the pressure, primary (wither scratching) and secondary positive reinforcers can be used to hasten relaxation. When I am loading difficult horses into the trailer I use "stop" and "go" pressures silently and keep my hands to myself (no patting). As

soon as the horse can step forward and stop in response to only light signals from the lead, then (and only then) do I begin to offer wither scratching. At this point you cannot overdo it, but if carried out earlier, caressing the horse will not hasten learning and may blur it.

Conditioned reinforcers: clicker training

Conditioned reinforcers have been used for many years in zoo animal training, and more recently have been adopted in dog and horse training.

Based on a technique initially pioneered by Skinner, this method pairs a food reward with a distinctive signal such as a whistle, a spoken word, a clicker, or even a flashing light. The signal becomes a "conditioned reinforcer" and bridges the gap between the performance of a behavior and the giving of a reward. Once the conditioned reinforcer and the food reward are strongly linked, the trainer can then use it to reward different behaviors the instant they occur.

Many trainers who use secondary reinforcers use a clicker (a small handheld device that makes a distinctive clicking sound), but any easily recognized signal can be used effectively. When using a conditioned reinforcer such as this for the first time it is important to pair the signal (the click) with the targeted repsonse and then the giving of the food reward. This is called "installing the clicker," and the timing of it is important. Once this has been repeated several times in fairly quick succession the conditioned reinforcer is said to be paired with the food reward and can now be used to train the horse.

Using the clicker is an easy way to train the horse to perform a simple behavior such as nudging a target with its nose. Hold the target in one hand in such a way that the horse is likely to sniff it or bump it with its nose, and hold the clicker in the other hand with a bowl of food rewards (such as carrots cut up into fairly small chunks) nearby. When the horse's nose touches the target, click and follow the click by giving a piece of carrot. Repeat, re-presenting the target, clicking each time the horse's nose touches it, and following every click with a food reward until the horse moves to touch the target with its nose as soon as it is presented. Once the conditioned reinforcer is strongly paired to the food reward it can be used to reinforce any desired. Behaviors that are reinforced are more likely to be repeated, and in this way many tricks and different behaviors can be trained.

The clicker could be of particular interest to dressage riders because it can be used to train behaviors from the ground and for shaping. The wastage rate of dressage horses is very high. Traditional training techniques rely heavily on the use of the whip to achieve movements such as piaffe (a highly collected trot, almost on the spot) and passage (an extremely elevated trot) and are sometimes very stressful for the horse. Clicker training could perhaps achieve or enhance results with less stress.

Classical conditioning

Classical conditioning (also known as Pavlovian conditioning) is the means whereby secondary reinforcements are learned by association. During this

Above *Research has shown that scratching and caressing the horse in front of the withers hastens relaxation.*

> *Any single event which coincides with a reinforced behavioral response will quickly become incorporated as a new cue.*

2 The trainer touches the horse's nose with the target and clicks at the same time. Clickers or whistles can be purchased. A children's toy beetle-clicker works fine.

1 Clicker training requires a target, a clicker, and food morsels such as apple pieces.

3 A food reward follows after the horse has touched the target and the trainer has "clicked."

4 Soon the horse will reach to touch the target wherever it is placed.

kind of learning a previously meaningless stimulus becomes linked to an event, and this is best illustrated by Pavlov's famous experiment.

Ivan Pavlov (1849–1936) was examining the interaction between salivation and the action of the stomach in dogs. In his experiment, a bell rang at the same time as he fed his dog, which salivated when it saw the food. In time the dog came to associate the bell with food, and began to salivate as soon as it heard it, whether food was offered or not. Pavlov called this a "conditioned reflex," and the process of learning it "conditioning." He also found that the conditioned reflex was repressed if the stimulus proved "wrong"

too often. If the bell rang repeatedly and no food appeared, eventually the dog would stop salivating every time it heard it ring.

Classical conditioning evolved in the wild to improve the efficiency of the animal's interaction with its environment. Any single event that coincides with a reinforced behavioral response will quickly become incorporated as a new cue: The sound of rustling bushes, preceding the appearance of a predator (and triggering the flight response) quickly becomes a cue for flight.

Classical conditioning can be a very useful part of training. However, it should never take the place of

operant conditioning, as responses that are trained by classical conditioning are not as stable as those trained by operant conditioning. Seat, voice, and weight signals are most often classically conditioned, but are only as effective as the operantly conditioned basics upon which they rely. The can certainly have influence, but they have no enforceable power.

In order to classically condition new cues, the cues must be given just before or during an established behavior. For example, if the rider wishes to train the voice aid "Whoa," the word should be spoken just before and overlapping the application of the rein signal for "stop." If the word is spoken after the reins are pulled, the new cue will not be learned. As the horse does not actually understand what "Whoa" means, but learns it as a cue, it must always be delivered with the same tone and pitch. Shouting it won't make the horse stop more quickly; only the conditioned version of the cue is meaningful to the horse. Repeating the cue quickly is ineffective too. The horse may perceive "Whoa, whoa, whoa" entirely differently from "Whoa," and it might elicit no response at all.

When horses learn to perceive the light version of the pressure signal that immediately precedes the stronger pressure, this is classical conditioning. In real life in the wild, and in domestic situations, classical conditioning and operant conditioning work together in forming learned responses in animals.

Habit formation

As the horse offers learned responses more automatically, it is said to be forming a habit. What is actually happening is that the behavior is moving away from the trial-and-error stage; the horse is no longer trialing various behaviors to remove the pressure, but is now reliably offering the "correct" one. The stability of the response results in consolidation of the neural pathways and networks that are unique for each learned response. The networks of the horse's brain are like a giant road map, where you can think of the freeways and highways as those habits that are well practiced, and the minor roads and tracks being the less practiced or unpracticed behaviors.

C. L. Hull, one of the all-time greats in the science of behavior, described habits as "a function of the number of reinforcements." In other words, it is the total number of stimulus/response units that is

responsible for the formation of habits, not the repetition of the behavior itself. (As we have seen, however, some behaviors such as flight response need fewer repetitions than others.) Hull's research indicates that it is most effective to train new behaviors in sets of between five and seven repetitions. Biometrics tells us that it takes thousands of repetitions of habits for them to become totally unconditional (when exactly the same habit will be elicited under all circumstances by the same stimulus). Martial arts and many other sports utilize this information by practicing habits for many years until they become reflexive. In horses we use the term "school horse" or "schoolmaster" to describe the horse that has a set of reliable habits in its training repertoire. When the horse has expressed a behavior as a result of a stimulus many times and for many years, it is harder to extinguish these habits. Thus, less experienced riders can be placed upon these horses and can learn the feel of certain trained movements without necessarily having all the skills it would normally take to produce and maintain them.

Our job in training horses involves being very clear about the importance of rapidly shrinking pressures to their lighter versions. If we try to avoid the use of pressure training we will ultimately confuse the horse, resulting in conflict behaviors that are detrimental to its welfare. Pressures are part of the life of the horse in social interactions between horses and their environment. It is therefore natural for the horse to learn to avoid pressures and learn predictive cues. In the next chapter we will examine the training principles that emerge from the science of learning.

Above Classical conditioning evolved in the wild to improve the efficiency of horses' interaction with their environment.

CHAPTER

5 THE PRINCIPLES OF TRAINING

TOM ROBERTS WAS A LEGENDARY AUSTRALIAN HORSE TRAINER WHO EXPLAINED NEGATIVE REINFORCEMENT TRAINING OF THE REIN AND LEG SIGNALS BY MEANS OF A "PROFIT-YOU/PROFIT-YOU-NOT" DIALOGUE. HE MAINTAINED THAT ONLY VERY LITTLE PRESSURE NEED BE USED, ESPECIALLY IN FOUNDATION TRAINING. IN RETRAINING, ANY STRONG PRESSURES RAPIDLY EVOLVE INTO LIGHT ONES. HIS WORDS EMBRACE THE AIMS OF GOOD TRAINING.

Of course, the demands of training are not so high if the aim is to do little more than trail ride, nose to tail. However, the training challenges presented by high-level performance horses are extreme. Rapid accelerations, decelerations, and turns are essential in most of these disciplines, and can all be achieved via pressure/release training.

Variable pressures applied by the rider's hands and legs are inevitable, and it is essential that horses are trained to react to tiny variations in pressure with a full range of possible responses. Matching signal strengths with response strengths is an important aspect of training because the exactness and consistency of the stimulus/response directly correlates with calmness and the degree of conflict behavior. Responses should mirror given signals.

Another essential aspect of correct training is that *only one response should be trained at any one time.* For example, training aspects of "stop" and "go" should be done on relatively straight lines rather than circles. Circles are turns, and so the horse is being expected to deal with two bits of information at once. Ignoring this interferes with training success, and may lead to the development of conflict behaviors. Even more importantly, go and stop signals should never be

Above and right *If trained correctly, stock and polo horses can accomplish rapid changes of speed and direction while remaining calm.*

Above *Tom Roberts is still remembered with great affection for his effective and subtle training techniques.*

issued simultaneously. Trainers should consider this when investigating the source of a behavior problem. As the horse's training consolidates, the two signals can be issued closer together, but never at the same time. Training is a matter of reducing all responses to their most basic components, and training them one at a time, particularly in the case of youngsters and problem horses.

Good, clear training results in calmness. Piet Wiepkema showed that when consistent signals lead to uniform responses, animals become free of tension, and their immune and digestive systems work at optimal levels. Our center weighs every week the horses that are sent to us for behavior modification. As soon as they are free of conflict behaviors, they begin to gain weight. They also socialize better, develop that contented "doe-eyed" look, and show a relaxed attentiveness to their surroundings; allegedly vicious colts and stallions transform into healthy, content individuals. This is the most rewarding aspect of our

business, and is, for me, what makes dealing with difficult and young horses eclipse any other equine training experience.

Our aim is to produce uniform responses so that the horse's behavior is the same each time it offers the response. When its legs or head and neck do different things in response to the same signal, the horse becomes confused. This can lead to problem behaviors and escalating fear. In nature, discrete stimuli elicit uniform responses; when responses become more variable, either the stimulus/response relationship diminishes, or the animal flees. For example, a bird call might herald the approach of a predator. The animal might respond, but if subsequent calls are not accompanied by the arrival of the predator, the animal's response diminishes. In social interactions, horses may flee the threats of other horses until the hierarchy changes, when the threats will no longer result in flight. Either way, our aim is that responses to stimuli become consistent.

The degree to which the horse expresses the flight response tends to be cumulative, especially in the early stages of its association with events. It may also get stronger each time it is expressed. By the time it is a well-established part of a horse's trained behavioral repertoire it can be extremely difficult to eradicate, and for this reason it should be dealt with in an error-free way. This means "deleting" expressions as they arise (see p. 60).

Our goal in training is to eliminate the effects of the environment (scary things, wind, other horses, and so on) on the behavior of the horse and place its behavior within the control system of signals elicited by the rider or handler. This is known as placing the behavior under stimulus control. Trainers need to establish signals that trigger consistent habits.

Everyone involved in any serious training of performance horses administers variations in pressure continually. After all, they have a set of reins in their hands connected to a super-sensitive mouth. While trainers concentrate on building up muscles to enable the horse to perform the desired task and "do its best," they don't always focus on the right things to ensure success. If they concentrated on correct

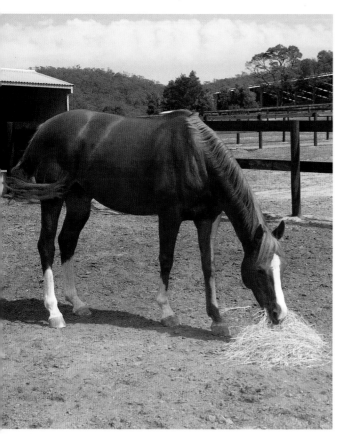

> *Everyone involved in any serious training of performance horses administers variations in pressure continually.*

installation and refinement of the pressure/release responses, their horses would suddenly appear far more physically adept and "willing to please." They would realize that reinstalling the most basic aspects of pressure/release responses one by one is the key to success with all behavior problems. Instead they focus on making the horse "want to please" them, and deliver multiples of signals, adding further to the blurriness of the horse's world, which was the cause of its problem in the first place.

Consider the notion that horses are "willing to please." Some horses do appear more willing than others, but this is because their genetics or past training propels them to trial the "right" behavior. Racehorses, jumpers, and dressage horses are really only demonstrating the interaction of their instincts and their training. Horses have better things to do (such as eat grass and be with their mates) than perfect their circle work and jump fences. The beauty of training is that when these jobs become habitual, there is every reason to suspect that performing them is rewarding to the animal (see p. 69).

This is why the word "training" is a more appropriate word than "teaching" with respect to human-horse interactions. "Teaching" implies subjective mental states, as if the horse is a willing partner in the exercise and understands its instinctive responses. As we have seen, the horse is neither willing nor unwilling; like other animals, it is "content" to form many different habits so long as these are clear, consistent, and without conflict.

Remember that training the horse to respond via negative reinforcement does not involve pain, but merely mild irritation if the horse has had correct training from the start. This irritation rapidly dissolves as the horse responds to light signals. With very difficult behaviors, stronger pressures are applied, but these are temporary and rapidly evolve to light signals. It is important to remember that it is not the pressure that trains, but the *removal* of the pressure. Trainers must reduce all signals to light signals for the horse to be free of conflict.

Left When a horse is free from conflict, it is easier to keep it healthy and in good condition.

THE PRINCIPLES OF TRAINING

Applying pressure

In early training or retraining, the range of possible pressures applied by lead rope, reins, or legs must be appropriate to the required response. Too much pressure can make the horse hyperreactive and activates the flight response; too little pressure can result in habituation to pressures and can lead to behavior problems. Pressure is most easily visualized as follows:

LEVELS OF PRESSURE

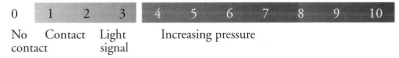

| 0 | 1 | 2 | 3 | 4 | 5 | 6 | 7 | 8 | 9 | 10 |

No contact | Contact | Light signal | Increasing pressure

Level 0 refers to the absence of contact: The lead rope or reins are looped; the legs are away from the horse's sides. In equestrian disciplines (other than Olympic and English ones), horses are mostly ridden on "no contact," that is, with loopy reins. In these sports, there is less potential for confusion because of rein contact. Negative reinforcement is most effective if pressure is reduced to level 0, or nil.

In Olympic and English disciplines, horses are trained and ridden on "contact": the reins are held with just enough tension to remain straight, and the legs hang gently against the horse's sides. Contact (level 1–2) is the light touch on the horse's head, mouth, and rib cage by the lead rope, reins, and rider's legs. The horse habituates easily to this level of pressure. As training progresses, the contact becomes more consistent. In horses that have been trained for sports other than Olympic or English disciplines, levels 1–2 of pressure are often sufficient to elicit a response; such horses have not habituated to contact, and so are responsive to very light pressure signals. Because "contact" has a specific meaning in some equestrian disciplines and can be problematic, I will use the term "connection" to describe the feel of the mouth through the reins and of the horse's body through the rider's legs.

The light signal (2–3) is the next level of pressure. When the trainer applies this in hand the connection is a more definite feel of the horse's head at the end of the lead rope. Under saddle the feel through the reins is "solid yet spongy," and the horse's rib cage feels snug to the rider's legs. The horse learns to respond to subtleties of these light pressures for various movements. This level always precedes the onset of stronger pressure.

The stronger pressure (4–10) builds up in intensity until the horse offers the correct response. In foundation training this stronger pressure should not need to be anything more than irritating, and in retraining (even in the most difficult cases of pressure habituation) stronger pressure is short-lived. If the pressure originates from a long whip, the speed (not the force) increases—the whip tap gets faster. As soon as the horse gives an improved, near correct, or correct response, the pressure instantly drops to 0.

When training a horse that offers no response, do not lessen the pressures (except for safety's sake) until it offers that response. When primary signals (see p. 56 and p. 58) fail and the whip is used, it is important not to stop the whip tap and go back to lead rope or leg alone. Softening the aid rewards the wrong response, and will add to the horse's confusion.

Signals and responses

If, for a moment, we think of the horse as a vehicle, we can see its capacity for movement in two dimensions. The horse has four legs, two at the front and two at the back. Its feet can go forward or backward. The forequarters can go sideways, right

Right *In Western, unlike European, training, horses are ridden with minimal connection between the rider's hands and the horse's mouth. As in all equestrian disciplines, the Western horse soon learns its cues from the rider's seat.*

and left; the hindquarters can go sideways, right and left. The forelegs turn when one leg slows relative to the other. The hindlegs turn when one leg produces more drive than the other. Every maneuver in every training discipline involves these movements, or combinations of them. The horse can go forward, backward, sideways with the forelegs, or sideways with the hindquarters. It can also go sideways with the forelegs and forward with the hindlegs, sideways with the hindlegs and forward with the forelegs, or sideways with both legs. It has the mobility of a hovercraft.

Perfecting such movement is the preoccupation of the sport of dressage, which evolved from war training maneuvers. The word "dressage" is French, from *dresser* meaning "to train." Dressage is the most complex of all the disciplines, with many variations of forward, backward, and sideways maneuvers, and very specific requirements of obedience, suppleness, gymnastic qualities, and physical outline of the animal. Most modern dressage horses today show a narrower training base because they rarely step

> *In early training or retraining, the range of possible pressures applied by lead rope, reins, or legs must be appropriate to the required response.*

outside the dressage arena; nevertheless, dressage represents the ultimate potential of captivating and signaling these responses in the horse.

The six basic horizontal directions of movement in the horse are elicited from different signals in hand and under saddle. In hand the signals are largely provided by the lead rope, whereas under saddle the responses are elicited primarily by the reins and the rider's legs. In dressage, eventing, and show jumping these signals are called "aids" (again derived from the French verb *aider*—to help). However, I will also use the words "signal" and "cue" in this book to accommodate all equestrian disciplines.

The signals used in foundation training to elicit the various movements of the horse **in hand** are:

- GO FORWARD, QUICKEN, OR LENGTHEN —lead rope pressured in forward direction
- STOP, SLOW, SHORTEN, OR GO BACKWARD —lead rope pressured in backward direction
- TURN FORELEGS RIGHT (TURN)—lead rope pressured forward and to the right
- TURN FORELEGS LEFT—lead rope pressured forward and to the left
- TURN HINDQUARTERS RIGHT (YIELD)— whip-tap pressure on left hindleg
- TURN HINDQUARTERS LEFT—whip-tap pressure on right hindleg

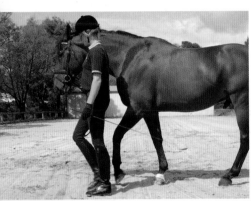

2 The horse must also learn to "park" (to stand immobile unless otherwise cued) and to step back from light pressure.

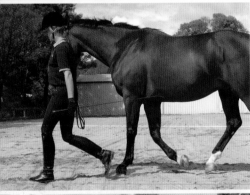

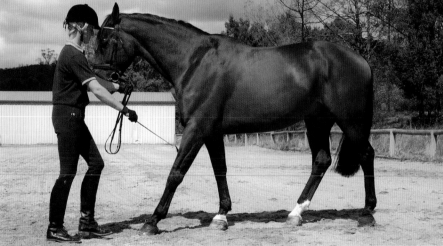

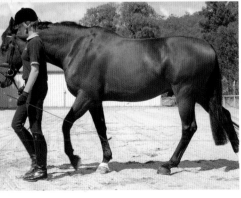

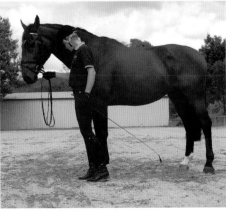

1 In hand, the horse learns to move forward from light lead pressure.

3 The horse learns to turn right when the handler's hand moves to the right.

4 The horse learns to turn left when the handler's hand moves to the left.

5 The horse learns to yield its hindquarters to the right from whip-tap pressure on the left hindleg.

« The primary signals should not be used for other purposes such as punishment. »

6 The horse learns to yield its hindquarters to the left from whip-tap pressure on the right hindleg.

The aim of training is to establish these responses from light versions of the signals. In the training of the turn of the hindquarters, the whip tap can eventually be replaced by light pressure of the fingers on the rib cage.

The signals that are trained *primarily* to elicit the various movements of the horse **under saddle** are:

- GO FORWARD, QUICKEN, OR LENGTHEN —pressure from both the rider's legs
- STOP, SLOW, SHORTEN, OR GO BACKWARD —pressure from both reins

- TURN FORELEGS RIGHT (TURN)—pressure from the right rein
- TURN FORELEGS LEFT—pressure from the left rein
- TURN HINDQUARTERS RIGHT (YIELD)— pressure from the rider's left leg
- TURN HINDQUARTERS LEFT—pressure from the rider's right leg

To be fully effective, it is essential that responses are uniform. At the earliest (and thus deepest) level of

1 Under saddle the horse learns to go forward from a light pressure from the rider's legs.

2 The horse learns to stop, stand immobile, and step back as a result of clear signals.

training, these signals must only produce the above responses. We are building one response at a time and one signal per response. Thus the forelegs are not brought to the left without the primary influence of the left rein. Going backward (otherwise referred to as "rein back") should initially be seen as a downward transition, a rein signal. Although later the legs can help cue the response by their backward *position*, training it from the legs at this early stage confuses the "go" action of the leg signals. This uniformity must be maintained especially carefully for young horses

To be fully effective, it is essential that responses are uniform.

3 *The horse learns to turn right from light pressure on the right rein.*

4 *The horse learns to turn left from light pressure on the left rein.*

5 *The horse learns to yield its hindquarters left from light pressure of the rider's right leg.*

6 *The horse learns to yield its hindquarters right from light pressure of the rider's left leg.*

Below and right The horse can be trained to stop and go from any signal—even the pressure of a light string around its neck can be used, with negative reinforcement, to elicit stop and turn signals.

Within half an hour I had trained the horse to stop and turn through the application and release of pressure of the string. In a few short sessions, using the negative reinforcement of the string, all aspects of the horse's stop response, head carriage, and turns were placed under new stimulus control and shaped, so that I could achieve all the (already installed) movements required for the Prix St. George dressage test. A bridle, however, is safer.

Ideally a unique signal should be attached to each response so there is no confusion for the horse. Pavlov showed that the stronger of two signals will dominate or "overshadow" the other. When presented separately, the weaker signal will get virtually no reaction. Overshadowing is a common failing of contemporary training systems where too many signals are used at one time for a single response. Even the tendency of trainers to "cluck" with their voice for just about every response blurs the effect of training to some extent. Many horses in competition are signaled to go forward with both spurs and whip, and appear to show diminished reactions. Such horses frequently do not have a forward response from either leg or whip separately.

Error-free training

This prevents the horse from making a habit of tension, and retrains an already tense horse. The instant tension shows in the horse, the rider signals an immediate downward transition. If, for example, the horse shows tension in trot, the rider should immediately do a downward transition to walk and then go forward again in trot. This "deletes" the incorrect behavior by not allowing the horse to practice it and so incorporate it into its repertoire. Alternatively the rider can give sufficient rein signals to slow the legs so that they maintain the slowest of steps without halting. After six or so of these, the rider may signal the horse to go faster.

In almost all training situations the most effective way to "delete" behaviors is to prevent them from being expressed. Riding the tense horse until it calms down (probably because it is tired) only allows it to practice being tense for longer periods of time. All behaviors that involve hyperreactive responses, that is, those related to the flight response, should be trained "error free." Horses that buck shouldn't be "ridden through" the bucking, but should be stopped

Above The horse refuses to jump—not because it has lost courage, but because its training has failed or it has received the wrong signals.

and/or horses that show problems in the responses. These basic associations lose their strength during the acquisition of problem behaviors, and a major aspect of remedial work is reconnecting these associations.

The system of signals used in horse training has developed because of ease, convenience, and safety. If done correctly, and using negative reinforcement, it is possible to train the horse to stop and go from any signal. At the Equitana horse festival I demonstrated how a horse without bridle or saddle could be controlled by a single piece of string around his neck.

1 After the horse has learned to initiate the go response, it is important to delete the flight response if that coincides with "go," so that the latter does not become reinforced. Here the rider performs an immediate downward transition.

2 This is then followed immediately by a reapplication of the "go" signal. The rider allows the horse to practice the correct behavior. The original tension was the result of an over-shortening of the neck. Now the task is to stop with a longer neck.

Right (clockwise from left) *Bucking develops as an incorrect response to the "go" signal. In bad cases, this is best deleted with an immediate downward transition, followed immediately by an upward transition. The rider leans back to ride a buck.*

or slowed and then immediately ridden forward, applying the "go" signal again. This should continue until the bucking ceases. Bucking is a "go" problem: Riding the horse through it just gives it the chance to perfect it. So downward transitions, followed immediately by firm "go" signals from the rider's legs, are the better solution.

Any movement that the horse performs that wasn't initiated by the rider should be deleted with a downward transition. All incorrect behaviors start with a loss of control over the horse's feet—the horse's legs either quicken or slow outside the rider's control—so the trainer should aim to have complete mastery of the horse's leg movements.

Riders often inadvertently allow the horse to perform incorrect behaviors that will affect later training. Allowing the horse to evade the basic signals by letting it walk off while being mounted ("stop" signal) or allowing it to sidestep puddles ("go" signal) can create "leakages" in the basic responses. These will show up when those responses are placed under pressure (such as at a horse show). Many riders become angry at their horse for rushing or shying in new situations without realizing that they have created the potential for those behaviors by allowing the horse to practice small versions at home.

Consistency and uniformity

It is not enough to expect the horse simply to travel forward, backward, or sideways. When we ask for forward the horse might go too fast or too slow. It might swerve or drift to one side. It might go with its head too high or too low, and drop the rein contact and shiver away from the rider's leg. These random behaviors need to be replaced with quantifiable, uniform behaviors.

Here is an easy way to think of how progressive control might work. Imagine that you have been given a wild horse and told to ride across the country, from point A to point B. You know nothing about horses, but you know the principles of training and can drive a car, so you set about your task with confidence.

The first thing you do is put on the bridle (you need to be able to stop the beast if it tries to run off with you). Next you start to habituate the horse to the sight of you jumping up beside it; if it moves forward you stop it. You stifle any expressions of the flight response and the horse rapidly habituates to this new stimulus. Soon you can sit up on it.

1 During mounting, the horse is prevented from moving forward through the maintenance of rein contact.

2 Random horse behaviors, such as deviating from the rider's line, should be corrected at "line and straightness" level (see p. 65).

3 Random behaviors in hand such as deviations in line should also be deleted with immediate downward transitions; or with slowing, where the horse is pushed back on line through appropriate rein contact.

Now begins the process of training it to go with a rider on its back. You must install brakes, an accelerator, and a steering wheel, which you do by careful application of pressure and release so that the right response is reinforced, and the wrong ones deleted. But you notice that when you pull on the reins and squeeze with your legs, the horse is slow to respond. This makes the rein signals heavy, like the brakes on your car when the power is off. The accelerator is also delayed and sluggish. You shape the responses so that they are expressed within a given time frame; now you have an immediate initiation of stop and go. But still you have no control over the animal's speed. It slows without warning and speeds up all by itself. Using the principles of error-free training you "delete" the random movements of the horse with transitions (changes of gait, up or down, or increasing or decreasing speed within the gait).

You notice that you now have cruise control, and later that the rhythm or beat of the horse's legs is even. But your horse is still swerving and drifting off your proposed line—it needs a wheel alignment! Using pressure of the left rein when it drifts right, then releasing as its forelegs respond by moving left, and vice versa, you gain control over the animal's direction, and (more or less) over its feet.

But it still shows moments of tension and raises its head too high, and sometimes it carries its head too low. Using rein pressures to slow it when it raises its head, and using leg pressures to quicken it when it lowers it, you now find you have a stable head carriage and a more constant connection to your reins and legs. The horse loses its hyperreactivity or tension.

Next you decide that it would be rather nice to have some "adjustability" within the gaits (rather than the horse dropping back to walk every time you use both reins at the trot, and popping into canter every time you use your legs). Now your controls are more subtle and you can use even finer signals to train some "adjustability" into the basic responses: You train him to lengthen and shorten his stride. You are also aware that this has made the horse feel more powerful and responsive.

Things are humming along beautifully when you come to a river crossing. All of a sudden it feels like the wheels have fallen off. The horse stops responding to your signals. It veers away from the water and now feels like it doesn't turn as well as before. As it turns, you notice its stop response has

1 When the horse raises its head it also hollows its back and shortens its stride as tension overwhelms its body.

2 When the horse lowers its head excessively, it usually loses speed.

3 The correct head position when walking on a long rein is with the poll at the highest point, just above the height of the horse's wither.

deteriorated too. You face it toward the water and use stronger turn pressures to prevent it from turning away, and maintain the pressure of your legs until it takes a step forward. You pressure for each individual step and reward with the removal of pressure. Eventually you are able to get the horse through the river. The next obstacle is a ravine and you experience similar problems, but this time they are resolved much more quickly. The animal's stop, go, and turn

1 When the horse resists a signal to go somewhere, such as into water, it slows and deviates from its line.

2 The rider quickly corrects forward and line deviations.

3 The rider should not allow the horse to avoid walls and corners.

4 The rider aims to train the horse to walk up the bank and out of the water calmly, maintaining a consistent rhythm.

5 Once the horse is able to step out of the water with a clear rhythm, the rider should be able to stop halfway up the bank.

> *Gradually, by tackling its random maneuvers one at a time, you make the animal more manageable.*

responses are now etched deeper into its brain—they are almost unconditional.

The point of this hypothetical exercise is to demonstrate the natural progression of training the basic responses, which is roughly what happens in foundation training. Gradually, by tackling its random maneuvers one at a time, you make the animal more manageable. We gain control by eliminating the worst things the animal can do first. It is also important that we train the animal to do what we want in a way it can learn, which means training one aspect of a particular response at any one time. Thus, shaping the final behavioral outcome of each of the responses is a matter of gradual refinement, which can be divided into seven stages:

Left and below When the horse trials incorrect responses due to losses of line and tension, it is important that the rider/handler does not reward the resulting behaviors by releasing the pressure that elicited them.

- basic attempt
- timing
- speed and rhythm
- line and straightness
- connection and outline
- adjustability
- proof

1 Basic attempt

At this first stage of training, the horse offers a rough response to the signals. The quality of the response doesn't matter: The important thing is that the horse does it. "Basic attempt" refers to the transition (the changes from one gait or one movement to another). The response may take some time to achieve in these early stages, but it is essential that the pressure is not released until the animal offers the correct response. If the horse gives an incorrect response and the pressure is removed, it will learn the wrong response. Similarly, if the horse gives a correct, or near correct, response, yet the pressure is not softened, it will not learn the stimulus/response connection. Training at "basic attempt" level is required for horses that buck, rear, offer opposing responses (such as going faster when the reins are pulled, slowing from the rider's legs, and pulling back from tethering), rear in hand, run away during leading or refuse to budge, pull the handler while being led, refuse to load into the trailer, rush off the trailer, refuse to enter the starting stalls, and refuse jumping obstacles (when not overfaced).

Sometimes, for safety's sake, compromises must be made where the response is virtually "set up" so that it can be elicited and then rewarded. For example, during foundation training under saddle, the very first step of forward is sometimes difficult to elicit. The turn of the forelegs is easier to produce, and so the handler can more easily elicit the forward response from the turn. During the training of forward in hand, pressuring the lead rope on a young or incorrectly

trained horse can sometimes lead to rearing, whereas pressuring the horse a little more sideways will alleviate this risk and still produce forward.

2 Timing

This refers to the speed of the horse's response to the rein or leg signal provided by the handler or rider. *There should be no delay in the initiation of the response.*

In the training of timing—often referred to as "obedience"—heavy pressure is transformed into light signals as the horse gives the correct response. All responses emerge in *three beats of the rhythm* of the gait. These coincide with the three events of pressure: first, a light signal; second, stronger pressure; third, the release of pressure. Why three beats? Because this

coincide with the three steps or three beats of the rhythm. This is repeated, and soon the horse reacts in a full-blown response from the light signal only. The three beats allow the horse to perceive the light signal. The trainer needs only to issue stronger signals occasionally when the horse makes an error or trials the wrong response, which happens less frequently as behaviors are consolidated. Even during the shaping of later qualities, the horse requires relatively light signals to correct errors because of this training in timing.

Timing is crucial in training yet has never been examined in equestrian literature. It is the key to the transitions flowing in an even rhythm within the sequence of the legs. Poor timing makes learning very difficult for horses and frequently leads to a range of behavioral problems. Horses with "hard mouths" that need strong bits, horses that are "lazy" and require spurs or a whip to maintain forward, and those that are heavy and dull to lead have not had clear training at this level. Most problems result in a deterioration of the timing of responses, and a subsequent loss of responsiveness to light signals, essential for the horse's calmness and well-being.

3 Speed and rhythm

Training the horse to maintain its own speed is essential. Many riders believe that they can hold the speed and rhythm or head carriage in their hands, but this generally causes stress in the horse (from pressure on its mouth) and confusion (through maintaining a degree of stop response without slowing or stopping). In such cases when the reins are let go, the horse quickens, and almost always shows a degree of tension. In all gaits the rider should be able to relinquish rein contact for a couple of strides without

Above During the training of the turn, the first beat of the rhythm is the inside foreleg. This must be initiated immediately by the horse from the light turn signal.
Right When the aids are consolidated, all the horse's gaits are relaxed, even the gallop.

has the effect of training both sides of the horse's body. Take the stop, for example, in walk. The light signal initiates a slowing leg. The stronger pressure enforces the opposite side to slow. The release occurs when the original foreleg now stops squarely beside the other. Squareness is a sign of a relaxed halt in correct timing and rhythm.

When assessing a horse I check whether or not the reins immediately initiate slowing, or whether my legs immediately initiate going forward or quickening. The same holds true for the turn responses and those in hand. I don't expect the animal to give the entire response rapidly, just to *initiate* the response rapidly. This tells me the degree of consolidation of responses: what the horse "knows" about the response.

At this stage the horse learns to respond from the light signal, perceiving that the light signal heralds the stronger pressure: The period of stronger pressure reduces to a single step (or single beat of the rhythm of the gait) as the horse learns to offer the response more readily. Then the trainer removes the pressure that coincides with the next step. Now the three phases of *light signal, stronger pressure, and release*

the horse losing speed or rhythm. This is only possible when timing has been trained correctly: Horses well trained in timing frequently exhibit self-maintained speed and rhythm. Not only does cruise control develop at this stage, but the transitions up and down between gaits become smoother and within the rhythm of the original gait.

In young or problem horses speed is trained initially by using pressure/release to produce changes in gait up and down. In persistent cases the quickening horse is slowed to the gait below, while the slowing horse is quickened to the gait above. In nonpersistent cases the horse may be just quickened or slowed within the gait.

This is also the stage where slower steps from the reins and faster steps from the legs are trained. These steps are produced continuously from light aids of leg or rein and maintained in a regular rhythm for a few steps. This begins the training of the half-halt.

Problems in speed and rhythm, as with those in timing, can lead to hyperreactive states, which may deteriorate to basic attempt problems.

4 Line and straightness

Once the horse can maintain its speed and rhythm in hand and under saddle, it is time to control its deviations of line: It must be trained to go where it is pointed. Wandering around is generally expected of young horses: It is a result of the random slowing or quickening of either of the forelegs, and the uneven drive of the hindlegs. But it is a training failure that, left uncorrected, can lead to more random behaviors.

Horses can deviate off line with either their forequarters or their hindquarters, and these should be treated as separate units in training. When horses being led drift to the side and "walk all over the handler," this is simply due to lack of training of line and direction. The horse is rewarded by such random behavior because it results in freedom, even if only for a stride or two; the more it swerves, the greater the freedom and the greater the reinforcement.

Training the horse to go forward and straight eliminates this behavior. Appropriate corrections of go and turn pressures eliminate line problems in hand and under saddle. Being able to make the horse slow and quicken obediently is essential to straightening. Line and straightness are well trained when the forelegs show no tendency to drift, and slight deviations of the hindquarters can be corrected with

1 At line and straightness level, the rider should correct any deviations of line with the rein signals, and then pressure the go signal harder on the side toward which the hindlegs are drifting. Here the horse has quickened from the pressure of the rider's leg and is resisting slowing by raising its head.

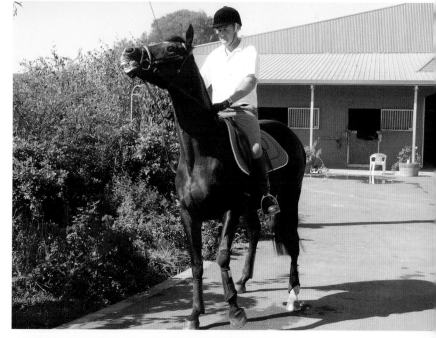

2 In-hand deviations of line should be corrected with downward transitions and with pressure applied away from the side toward which the horse drifts.

1 Forcing the horse's head position by using stop and go pressures applied simultaneously will create tension and invite conflict behaviors.

2 When the horse is correctly trained it will maintain a relaxed and uniform head carriage.

" *The horse associates a high head carriage with the flight response and hyperreactivity.* "

light leg signals. A straighter body emerges when drift is eliminated. Line is the precursor to straightness.

5 Connection and outline

The horse's legs are now under control in all directions, but still there may be variations in connection to the lead rope, reins, or rider's legs, in the horse's carriage, and in its body tension.

The "outline" of the horse—the carriage and posture of the head and neck—is as important in hand as under saddle. It is intimately related to the connection of the rider to the horse (the constant feel of the reins on the horse's lips and tongue, and of the rider's legs on the horse's rib cage). "Connection and outline" is the precursor in dressage training to "contact."

The horse associates a high head carriage with the flight response and hyperreactivity, and a low head carriage with calmness. A high head carriage is generally linked with short, quickening steps and a low head carriage with slowing steps. A low head also redistributes more weight to the forequarters of the horse, resulting in stalling. Hyperreactivity is sometimes associated with an unsteady connection to the lead rope, reins, or rider's leg. Depending on whether the change in posture results in quickening or slowing, appropriate downward or upward transitions are used. This trains the horse to maintain a relaxed head carriage. Lowering the horse's head carriage with the reins is feasible only during a downward transition or slowing response because of the risk of disconnecting the rein signal from the slowing response. The head carriage is raised with appropriate transitions.

Horses with problems at this level are said to be "on the forehand" or "hollow in the back," depending on whether the head is carried too low or too high. When the horse is correctly trained in connection and outline, its basic training is more or less consolidated.

6 Adjustability

The horse has already learned to respond *faster* and *slower* from the leg and rein signals. When fast steps are elicited from light signals and can be maintained in rhythm, stride length emerges naturally. Similarly slower steps evolve to beome shorter. Now we can address the question of stride length. Adjustability involves the training of the longer and shorter strides in three beats of the rhythm, or in three steps of the gait. This is the precursor to collected and extended qualities of the gaits.

7 Proof

Dog trainers use this term to describe training the dog to respond in the same way to the same signals unconditionally. This is equally important for horse training because horses, as a prey species, are even more susceptible than dogs to environmental distractions including sights, sounds, and the presence of other horses. The more inexperienced the horse, the more likely it is to lose some of its trained responses when first taken out of the training environment. These have to be reinstalled one by one in the new environment.

"Proof" should be trained gradually. I have found that it takes about five different environments to consolidate a reliable response; for example, it takes training over five different water obstacles to result in most horses not balking as they approach a novel one. This is not hard to explain if you imagine five different photographic negatives of five different water jumps. When viewed one right after the other, the only common denominator would be the water. Remember, however, that it will take many more than five repetitions if the horse does not show uniform or correct behavior on completion of each trial.

Self-carriage

A guiding principle in all correct training systems is that of self-carriage. This means that the training of all the previously described qualities must result in the horse itself maintaining *its own* rhythm, speed, line, straightness, connection, and outline at every stage. The rider should be able to release rein and leg contact for a couple of strides without losing any of these qualities. Most equestrian disciplines fall short of this principle.

The three Rs

As you may have guessed by now, horses do not learn things by sudden "realizations." Instead, three factors affect the speed of learning:

Repetition

Some habits die hard. In general, the younger the behavior, the faster it modifies; the less practiced it is, the quicker it can be replaced by other behaviors. The number of times a behavior has been expressed or repeated influences its persistence and likelihood to result again from the same stimulus. This is simply the power of habit formation in action. A particular behavior, however, is not just a product of the number of repetitions; in some cases, it takes only a few repetitions to acquire a learned response. Fear responses, for example, have been known to become installed in the horse in just one trial. For an explanation of this we need to look at the next "R."

Reinforcement

What makes a new behavior likely to be repeated is the degree to which it is reinforced, or rewarded. Food, freedom from pressure, and so on tend to reinforce the behavior that brought them about.

Most horse people know that it only takes a rider to be bucked off a horse a couple of times to make a repetition of this behavior likely. This is because any expression of the flight response significantly reinforces any behavior associated with it. The horse that is able to kick and thrash its way to freedom will experience such behavior as highly reinforcing. Thus it takes far fewer repetitions to install shying, bucking, bolting, rearing, and general tension (in hand and under saddle) than other behaviors. The strength of the reinforcement is an important factor in determining the likelihood of repetition.

Recency

The more recently an animal has performed a behavior, the more likely it is to be elicited again. Research has validated the practice of training each day, with maybe a break on the weekend. Horses seem to retain information better if trained regularly without long gaps between sessions.

A change in behavior will be more effectively installed if the response is trained "close together." When animals canter or gallop, there is a "leading leg": One foreleg is noticeably leading the others and seems to stretch out further. On a circle the leading leg should be the inside foreleg, as in nature. When animals change direction they do a flying change: They swap from one leading leg to the other.

In most training disciplines the leading leg is elicited on demand from a combination of rein, seat, and leg signals. However, some horses become habitual in their leading leg and favor one only. This habit can be altered if the "non-favorite" leading leg is immediately re-signaled once it has been practiced by the horse for a certain number of strides, and the horse then brought back to the trot for a couple of strides. Spacing the new behavior close to the previous behavior for a number of sessions makes a significant difference to the speed of its acquisition.

A note on the fear response

Animals can entirely forget some behaviors through "extinction": You can train a rat to press a lever or a pigeon to peck a key pad, and by altering reward schedules you can make them forget their original behaviors (or at least confuse these with other novel behaviors). But this is not the case with fear.

Joseph le Doux has demonstrated convincingly that fear behaviors are exempt from extinction or "forgetting." However, this information completely passed the horse industry by; at the time, techniques of catching wild horses by chasing them in round pens were being reinvented, hailed as ground-breaking, and marketed for their kindness! The advocates of this technique justify it on the following grounds:

- *It is an emulation of the stallion-herd dynamics.* This is a deeply flawed argument: It is inconceivable that a horse would regard a human as a horse.
- *The end justifies the means.* But if the means involves inflicting permanent damage through installing stored fear, then this argument too is invalid.
- *The horses "understand" their respective actions, and make conscious choices to approach, "negotiate with," and accept the human.* This seems most unlikely. Round-pen work is simply another form of negative reinforcement where the horse discovers the impossibility of escape. Meanwhile, the trainer negatively reinforces slowing and approaching through the on-and-off aversive actions of chasing. Consider the case of a cat who constantly thwarts the escape of a mouse it is "playing" with. Eventually the mouse chooses not to run away

anymore, because escape is futile. Would anyone suggest that the mouse now chooses to be with the cat, that the cat is now "family?"

- *It results in the horse approaching rather than running away from the handler.* This is certainly a useful outcome, but there are other, less invasive means to train it (see p. 84).

Chasing fearful horses in this way should be stopped. The horse never forgets any interaction with a human that produces this degree of tension and hyperreactivity. From a neurological point of view the pathways between the stimulus (the human) and the response (fear) are strengthened, and this may well affect other behaviors.

Techniques such as lungeing and chasing in the round pen that may appear to be harmless from a human perspective may unintentionally harm the horse in the long term. But it is important to note that these actions are damaging only if the horse shows hyperreactive (fear) responses. If the horse lunges calmly, drives calmly, or is not fearful of being chased, this argument does not apply. However, such "chasing" is likely to induce fearful behavior and tension in young or naive horses. In older, calm horses, lungeing may be used successfully to assist in various aspects of dressage training.

Adding new signals

Once the horse has well-established basic signals that have been trained via negative reinforcement, the rider can add other classically conditioned cues such as seat, weight, and voice. However, no matter how far the horse's training progresses, it should always be able to demonstrate good, clear responses to the signals that were trained with negative reinforcement. If these basics are maintained, and providing riding skills and balance are adequate, the horse will be far less likely to manifest conflict because it has clear boundaries and consistency to its behaviors.

Trainers should remember that classically conditioned signals (such as voice commands) are not enforceable in themselves—they are only as effective as the operantly conditioned signals upon which they rely, and should not be introduced until these are dependable and established. Another important point is that if two strong signals are used (such as leg pressure and whip pressure for forward), each should

> *Animals can entirely forget some behaviors…*
> *But this is not the case with fear.*

be trained separately as well for maximum effect. The horse should learn through negative reinforcement to go from the whip alone so that it eventually goes, and remains going, from just a single light tap. When used together, the signals should always be light leg followed by whip tap. It is also worth remembering that horses readily learn classical conditioning as they perceive much information from surrounding events. Thus it is really not necessary to train the seat, weight, or body-position signals—the horse learns them anyway provided the rider has correct posture.

When the horse exhibits clearly trained responses to the rein and legs, the use of the seat presents a new and challenging frontier. Because the horse is now fully operational from light signals, the seat and weight aids can be used to great effect in achieving greater harmony between horse and rider. When seat and weight aids fail, rein and leg responses have likely deteriorated as well.

When the horse moves forward, its back moves, and these movements are different in each gait. The rider's seat is influential in maintaining the horse's rhythm, and the skillful rider aims to move in exact synchrony with the horse. This skill has been the preoccupation of various riding traditions for centuries. The best riders have the ability not only to move with the horse, but to move a little ahead of or a little behind the horse's movements, and in this way to control its rhythm.

The trainer

The good trainer is objective and does not allow emotion to enter the training context in a negative way. He or she is able to isolate the exact moment that the young or difficult horse offers the desired behavior and release the pressure accordingly. Good trainers of well-established horses must always issue clear signals, and back them up with a little more pressure if the horse offers only a diminished response, or no response at all. They should be careful not to disconnect primary responses from their signals. For example, the reins should not be used for responses other than stopping or turning unless these primary responses are included in the signal. Thus the reins should not be used to alter the horse's head carriage *unless* the horse is slowing.

Trainers need to ask themselves questions such as: "What rewards this behavior?" and "Is my training system (or am I) effective enough?" rather than hide behind excuses such as: "This horse comes from a long line of useless, good-for-nothings and spends its days thinking up ways to wreck my life."

The rider

The rider must be balanced and relaxed, able to apply the signals in a consistent and uniform manner, and to maintain a stable body position despite any sudden movements that the horse may make. There are many specialist texts on improving rider position and stability. Trainers should make a careful study of these as it is certainly useful for all riders to have a thorough theoretical knowledge of correct position.

Correct rider position is not just a form of arena etiquette; it fosters stability and consistency, and allows the pressure/release signals to be applied in the same place on the horse's body every time, regardless of what the horse is doing.

There is a tendency among horse riders to equate the difficulty of a horse with the skill level of its rider, so when a horse is being particularly difficult it is often assumed that the rider is particularly talented. In fact, the opposite is quite often true: Difficult horses are usually being trained and ridden in conflict and inadvertently rewarded for practicing incorrect

Below *Correct rider position allows aids to be applied in a uniform way.*

behavior. While quiet, calm, and obedient horses are almost always far better trained than tense, difficult ones, it is also true that a quiet horse is not necessarily an obedient one. A quiet horse may sometimes be less trainable than a more sensitive animal, particularly if it shows hyperreactive responses to girth pressure or tends to trial incorrect responses to leg pressure.

Horses are individuals

Robert Miller's work on imprinting and early learning in horses tells us that they are capable of learning from the moment of birth. He encourages the correct handling of foals at an early age, when less able to use strength against humans. He shows that foals are capable of learning in-hand work, and can habituate and become desensitized to stimuli.

Of course there are great variations in horses in terms of sensitivity, in their propensity to show hyper-reactive responses. However, what horsemen often regard as "intelligence" in horses needs careful qualification. Clearly there are some that learn certain tasks very quickly, while others are slower. The "hotter" breeds such as the Arabians and Thoroughbreds are generally supposed to be quicker on the uptake, while the "colder," less sensitive heavier breeds and the warmbloods (crosses between the "colder" and the "hotter" breeds) are generally regarded as slower.

Intelligence, however, is how you measure it. Motivation is relevant in any test of intelligence. Sensitive horses are highly motivated to trial responses that alleviate any pressure they are exposed to, so in typical training, these horses appear much smarter than the others. When the motivation is changed,

however, the results are interesting. During my experiments in equine mental abilities, I used food as a motivator, and the "dumb-bloods" (the equestrian nickname for warmbloods) did just as well as, or better than, the other breeds. Less sensitive horses generally require a little more pressure than the more sensitive breeds to motivate them to offer responses.

It's also true to say that some horses appear destined to be perfect, and are universally described as "willing to please." These horses, however, are the ones that tend to trial the "right" behavior. There is every reason to suspect that we are selectively breeding such horses because those that trial the right behavior tend to be successful, and therefore go on to stud.

Another consideration relates to the physical capabilities of individual horses. Some horses are simply more mechanically suited to some sports than others, by virtue of their conformation. This impacts upon training success and on the welfare of individual horses: Some are never going to be capable of doing certain things. Thoroughbreds, quarter horses, and Arabians are generally more suitable for contests that involve speed. For endurance capabilities, Thoroughbreds and Arabians predominate. For sports involving power, such as show jumping and dressage, warmbloods, warmblood crosses, and heavier crosses tend to be most suitable. Sports that require a mixture of power and speed, such as cutting horse and games competitions, generally require lighter-framed horses such as quarter horses and various crossbreds.

The differences in conformation between the powerful and fast horses can be seen primarily in the ratio of height of wither (the topmost point of the

Right *Heavier breeds such as the warmbloods and draft type breeds (near right) are generally higher at the wither than the croup. This trait is useful for the power required for jumping and dressage. On the other hand, speed is conferred by a croup that is higher than the wither (far right).*

shoulders) to croup (the topmost point of the pelvis). Horses that require power tend to be higher in the wither than the croup; those that require speed generally have higher croups than withers. A higher croup allows the forces of propulsion of the hindlegs to be exerted in a more horizontal plane, whereas the higher wither allows the forces to be exerted in a more vertical plane. This direction of force allows the draft horse, the jumping horse, and the dressage horse to derive necessary power. Sprinting racehorses and quarter horses show the greatest development of the higher croup to wither.

Health and safety considerations

There are many excellent texts available on safe handling and riding practices, and anyone involved with horse training should be thoroughly familiar with these. A well-fitted approved safety helmet is important, regardless of the discipline. Ropes and lead ropes should never be looped around the body or limbs. When training young or problem horses on the ground, an enclosed, safely fenced yard or arena is useful. The training surface should be relatively flat and the footing safe.

All equipment used in handling or riding should be maintained in a safe manner and the stitching of saddlery checked for wear on a regular basis. Although modern saddlery stores are filled with gadgets of every shape and size, the gear required for training is relatively simple. A well-fitted leather or rope halter is ideal for most in-hand work, while an anti-rearing bit can be used for more difficult problems. A safe, well-maintained snaffle bridle and saddle (of any kind) are necessary for training under saddle; the most important requirement is that they fit well and suit the horse and rider. The long whip should be firm and not too long or heavy so that the trainer may easily apply it in a rapid tap-tapping motion.

Trainers and riders should have the health of their horses checked regularly; pain compromises training, and it is unethical and unfair to work a horse that is uncomfortable. The horse should have its teeth checked by a veterinarian at least twice a year between the ages of two and five, and once a year after five years of age. Low-grade unsoundness of the limbs may compromise the horse's training, as will conformation that is unsuitable for the desired discipline. Riders should work closely with their

Left The equipment required for effective training is simple, but it must be safe and well maintained. Approved safety hard hats are essential for safe riding.

veterinarians and other health professionals in order to maintain the horse in optimum condition.

Trainers throughout the ages have learned the secrets of success through trial and error, yet their explanations defied their skills. Today's exponents, armed with a knowledge of the cognitive sciences, have a great advantage. It is now possible—even imperative—for them to refine their methods so as to integrate scientific theory into modern training systems. The shaping process outlined here, from Basic attempt through to Proof, is one of gradual refinement aimed at reducing aspects of training to single, trainable qualities that the horse can learn, one at a time. We are now ready to look at training blueprints, in hand and under saddle, that naturally emerge from a knowledge of equine learning and the principles of training.

CHAPTER 6 IN-HAND TRAINING

IN-HAND TRAINING—CONTROLLING THE HORSE BY SIGNALS FROM THE LEAD ROPE, OR REINS IF WEARING A BRIDLE—DOES NOT INVOLVE WINNING BATTLES FOR DOMINANCE, EVEN WHEN WORKING WITH A STALLION OR WITH WHAT SOME MIGHT CALL A "ROGUE" HORSE. IT COMES DOWN TO USING THE POWER OF REINFORCEMENT TO MODIFY THE HORSE'S BEHAVIOR, AND MAKING THE TRAINING PROCESS SIMPLE ENOUGH FOR THE ANIMAL TO LEARN.

The aim of in-hand training is to produce a horse that performs a range of maneuvers—leading forward; stop and slow; turn; and moving hindquarters in either direction—from light signals and with a fluid rhythm. It should hold its line without drifting, maintain a light but permanent connection with the trainer, remain calm in the body, offer the requested stride, and go wherever and whenever the trainer decides. When the horse has all these qualities, the consistency and uniformity of its responses to quiet signals renders it calm.

I do not intend to promote one particular "method" of training. No one has yet developed the perfect system, and relying on only one method can be limiting, locking one into traditional training systems to be followed without question. The challenges of modern equestrian sport are constantly changing in line with fads and fashions in horses and competitions. Modern trainers need to be versatile and objective. But any good training system should follow the fundamental principles of learning and reinforcement.

This chapter covers the basic training tasks of leading, catching, tethering, shoeing, loading into the

Left *For safe and effective in-hand training, the handler requires an approved helmet, safe footwear, and a long whip. The horse should be in a bridle or halter with possibly a rubber rearing bit.*

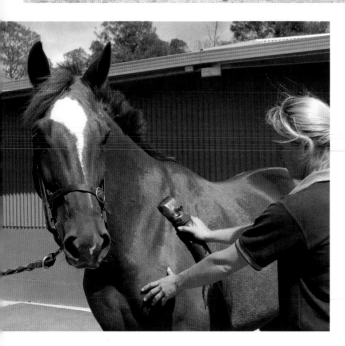

Above *Effective in-hand training makes all the difference between a calm safe horse during activities such as clipping...*

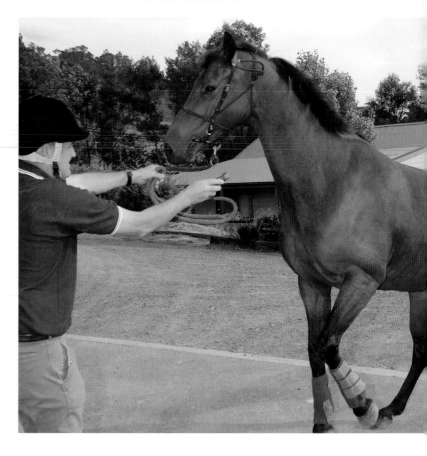

trailer, and loading into race stalls. Once clear responses are well established it is a relatively simple matter to train other in-hand behaviors, and the daily handling and management of the horse becomes problem free.

The equipment used for in-hand training is simple. At the most basic level it requires only a lead rope attached to the halter. Many people prefer to use a rope halter because the thinness of the noseband/headpiece makes it potentially more aversive than a wide leather or webbing halter, and tends to result in the horse "trialing" responses more readily. The use of a long whip greatly assists in achieving responses because of its clear tap-tapping action. It should never be used in punishment. Those who criticize the whip do so because they misunderstand its correct use.

Left and above … *and one that is terrified of clippers. The horse has learned that panic makes the holder of the clippers retreat. Curing this involves habituating the horse to the clippers and deepening the "go" and "stop" responses.*

> *Those who criticize the whip do so because they misunderstand its correct use.*

Because the whip tap is useful in in-hand training, it is important that the horse is not fearful of it. Habituation is achieved by laying the whip gently on the horse and preventing it from moving its legs using the pressures of "stop" and "go" appropriately and clearly. As the horse becomes calmer, the habituation session should be repeated until the horse can stand calmly while the whip caresses its body. The whip should never alarm the horse; if it does, it usually means that someone has used too much force and/or incorrect application and timing. Under no circumstances should the whip leave the body if the horse shows signs of hyperreactivity: This simply reinforces the response. Instead it should be held against the body until the horse is calm.

Most horse trainers wear gloves, helmet, and boots. Many insist that their employees wear a back protector for all horse-handling activities. *Trainers should remember that in-hand training has associated risks.* Safe training means wearing an approved safety helmet and taking care to stand on one side of the horse, not directly in front of it, at all times.

Both in-hand and under-saddle training, in the early stages, are conducted mostly at the walk, using the transitions from walk to stop, stop to backward, backward to walk, and occasionally walk to trot. Immobility is also an essential feature of training.

Forward

The first task is to train the Basic attempt (see p. 65), or crude response. Let's imagine that the horse has no experience of the lead forward response or the stop/slow response from pressure signals of the lead rope. Consequently, no amount of pressure results in the horse moving forward. The problem is not that the horse can't or won't go forward, but that the stimulus the trainer is applying does not elicit the response. The horse does not "know" what is required, even if it seems fundamentally clear to the trainer.

When this happens trainers often move to one side so that the horse is pressured to move sideways

and forward. This is achieved by standing in front and slightly to the side and increasing the pull on the lead rope, then releasing it as soon as the horse offers a single step toward the handler. It works because it is relatively easy to unbalance the horse sideways.

The sideways steps of the horse are repeated again and again. The trainer must ensure that the horse is rewarded for stepping a single step at first, then a complete stride (one foreleg followed by the other). Soon the trainer can begin to pressure the horse more forward than sideways. Remember that whatever behavior the horse offers, the pressure is softened only when the horse gives the desired response. The reinforcing aspect of training is the removal of the pressure; it is important, therefore, that it is *removed*

Below *To test and initially train "go," face the horse holding the reins short. Initiate the "go" response with the light rein signal, then use the whip if required. When speed and rhythm are achieved from a light signal, face the same direction as the horse.*

Stop

Once the horse moves forward from a pressure cue it is time to train the stop/slow responses. Until this point horses are often quite sluggish in their forward responses, so stopping tends to happen without a signal from the handler. The horse is ready to learn to stop when the timing of the forward response (immediate, and from light signals) is more or less reliable.

Consider what stopping and slowing actually entail. The legs slow down (or, to use the metaphor of the car again, come down a gear). Reversing simply represents a further going down of the gears from stop. Reversing is the most useful training tool for many incorrect random behaviors, hyperreactive

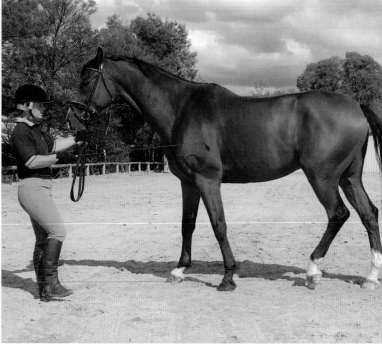

"The horse is beginning to learn that light pressure precedes an increase in pressure, and the responses become more immediate."

entirely every time the horse complies. The horse is beginning to learn that light pressure precedes an increase in pressure, and the responses become more immediate from light versions of the signals.

behaviors in particular, so it is essential that it is trained early and clearly. Remember that only a single step is necessary at first; if two are asked for then the first one is unrewarded, thus confusing the horse. Multiple steps backward must be asked for only if they can be elicited from light signals; if still requiring heavier signals, each step is requested individually.

Horses can usually be stimulated to step backward by pressuring the lead rope toward the neck. If the lead-rope pressure elicits no response, this light signal can be combined with tapping a foreleg with the long whip and later the chest. If the trainer is sensitive to releasing

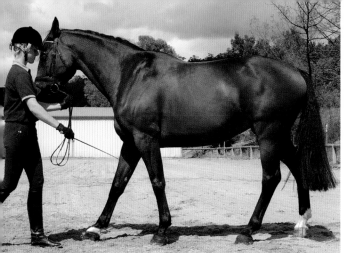

1 *To deepen stop, train a step back. A mild rein signal is followed by a leg tap if the horse is slow to step back or does not respond to the lightest signal.*

> *Any delays in the horse's responses are corrected with increasing pressure followed by rapid release at the moment of the response.*

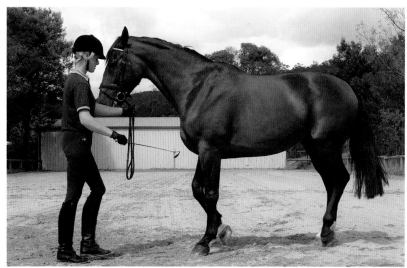

2 *In five or so repetitions the horse will step back from the light pressure only, and the whip will become increasingly redundant.*

pressure the very instant the horse offers a correct response, strong pressures will be unnecessary. We want the horse to learn to step backward in response to the light posterior pressure of the lead rope, so that must be signaled before any other pressure. The stop response is trained through the single backward step. As soon as the Basic attempt occurs fairly reliably the timing of the response should be trained. Any delays in the horse's responses are corrected with increasing pressure (perhaps combined with faster tapping on the legs) followed by rapid release at the moment of the response. This transforms the stop signal to a lighter version through classical conditioning.

Now it is a matter of repetitions to consolidate the stop response at this level. When this happens, speed and rhythm tend to follow automatically, especially in foundation training. In retraining, speed and rhythm aspects may need further modification.

Refining go and stop responses

This can be done through the use of transitions so that ultimately the horse performs these consistently, and maintains speed and rhythm; line and straightness (so that any swerving is eliminated); connection to the handler (via the lead rope); and head and neck carriage. It should also be adjustable (able to take longer and shorter steps) and obedient to the responses in any circumstance. These are all achieved through up

3 *Soon the handler can face the same direction as the horse. To test the rein response, the handler stops the horse before slowing down herself. Here the handler is in the correct leading position, where stop and go signals can be administered easily.*

Right *With foals and naïve horses the very first step forward should be initiated by mild sideways pressure. Clear release after a single stride (one foreleg followed by another) is essential to quick learning.*

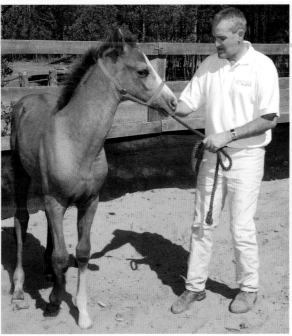

or down transitions. Behaviors that incorporate random slowing or stalling, including drifting and head-carriage changes, are corrected with upward quickening transitions. Behaviors that incorporate random quickening, including some instances of head-raising, are retrained with downward slowing transitions. In retraining it is sometimes especially useful to train a deeper go response by quickening and lengthening the horse's stride. This can be done with the use of a thinner rope halter where the horse is

pressured to make a single step slightly sideways as it is traveling forward. This enables the relatively weaker human to elicit a faster and longer step. Another way is to apply lead pressure for forward then tap the horse's rib cage with the dressage whip. The end result should be that greater pressure applied to the halter should result in a quickening and eventually a trotting from increases in lead pressure only. Similarly if the horse quickens or slows easily it can be trained to lengthen and shorten within the gait. When the horse

Right *Train the horse to quicken its steps as a result of light lead pressure by escalating the pressure so that it steps to the side more quickly for one step only (inside foreleg) while it is walking forward. This deepens the go response.*

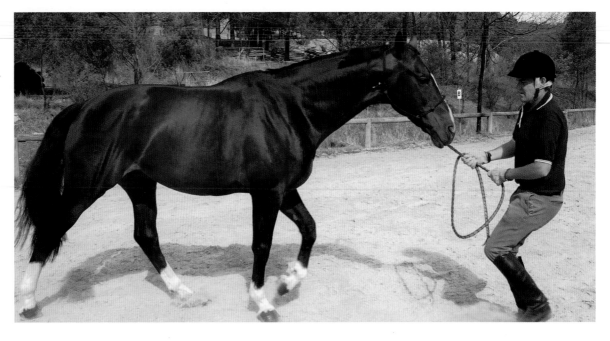

responds to light signals, the trainer can face the same direction. The correct position is beside the horse's head; otherwise stop, go, and turn signals can be effected.

Standing still

Once stop and go are established it is time to train the horse to stand immobile, which is easily done through pressure/release. We sometimes refer to this as training the horse to "park" (rather like "stay" in the dog). If the horse steps forward, it is immediately stepped back to its original position; if it steps back it is stepped forward, if it steps sideways, it is stepped back. Sideways steps can be considered the same as forward steps because if the horse were free of the lead rope influence it would have stepped forward and departed the situation. However, the influence of the lead pressure partially thwarts this response and the horse steps sideways instead.

Training the turn

Training the horse to turn its forelegs in hand is very simple because there is only one lead rope. The stimulus is slightly different from the normal lead forward stimulus in that it is slightly to the side: The hand of the handler indicates the direction of the turn. The horse feels extra pressure from the lead rope/halter on the opposite side of its face. The turn response can be refined in the same way as the go and stop responses.

Head down

It is useful to train the horse to lower its head on cue. This has a calming effect: The horse is very good at making associations, and this posture recalls pleasant pastimes such as grazing. Lowering the head can help to calm a nervous horse, but one should be careful that the technique is not used as a band-aid for dealing with hyperreactivity caused by poor responses. But the most important aspect of training the head down response is that it deepens the yielding of the horse to pressure in general.

The response can be trained using downward pressure of the rein. Always keeping its head well clear of the horse's, the trainer applies pressure downward, then releases the pressure the instant the horse makes the Basic attempt and lowers even just a little. It is important that the trainer does not release the

pressure until the horse lowers its head, even if only marginally. The horse should eventually be trained to lower its nose to the ground, although it will be quite erratic at this early stage.

Gradually the horse is trained to respond more quickly by increasing the downward pressure after the initial lowering. By being accurate in the timing of the release and using stronger pressure when the response is heavy, the horse will soon lower its head from a light touch, and can be trained to keep on lowering all the way to the ground. Soon the rhythm of the lowering is smooth. Next to be trained is the straightness of the head and neck, so that the horse learns that the response is not connected with a neck that is bent in any lateral way. At this stage the connection of the lead rope to the horse should be smooth and even. If it is not—if there are any variations in pressures from the light signal—repetitions must be performed until the signal is smooth and continuous. Now the horse is trained to speed or slow the response according to the signal provided. Finally the horse is trained to perform these responses anywhere and everywhere it is asked.

Yielding hindquarters

The horse's hindquarters can be trained to turn sideways from whip-tap pressure. This can be classically

81

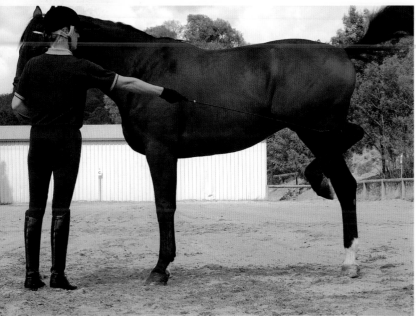

opposite leg. The trainer removes the pressure of the tapping whip as soon as the horse makes a step. The horse may attempt to move forward but must be prevented from doing so.

This is practiced until a single tap results in the horse crossing its left hind over its right hind at the level of the fetlock. The timing is now on its way to becoming reliable. The next thing to be trained is the eliciting of another step by the light single tap, then another. This is the speed and rhythm aspect. Next the horse should be held perfectly straight so that there are no confounding and inconsistent aspects to this training caused by a crooked neck. Connection and outline are now trained. This is necessary because the horse may raise its head when first tapped and may incorporate this into the reaction. At this stage also the contact of the lead rope may still be a little heavy. This

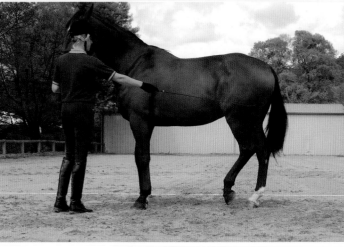

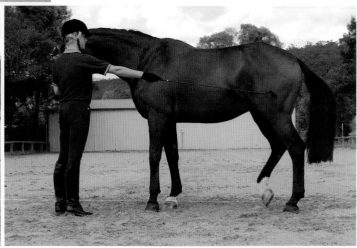

Above *Turn of the hindlegs is achieved by tapping until the horse steps across. Soon it steps across smoothly from a single light tap.*

conditioned so that eventually the response is elicited from a light finger-pressure cue on the horse's rib cage.

With whip taps, it is important to separate the area on the horse's body that relates to "forward," and the area that relates to sideways yielding of the hindquarters. The shoulder is the most convenient place to tap it for forward in hand, but in reality it can be anywhere from the flank to the shoulder, but *never* the flank itself. For yielding it is the sides of the rump, but *never* the flank. The flank is too sensitive and tapping with the whip there is too punishing. This will make it clear to the horse which direction is wanted. Facing the horse's near side (left side) the trainer holds the whip in his right hand and the horse in his left, and taps it continuously on the hock joint until it steps a little away from the whip toward its

stage must be practiced with slightly stronger lead pressure until the head and neck placement is consistent. Next the steps are further pressured using the whip tap to encourage longer steps (crossing at hock level). Finally the response is tested and trained in other environments. Ultimately a single light whip tap should result in the full-blown sideways response.

If the trainer perfects these maneuvers so they end up resulting from light aids the whip will become unnecessary. The trainer will be able to tap the horse further up the hindquarters, closer to the rump. This response should be trained equally on both sides. Eventually the tapping of the whip can be replaced with the pressure of one finger behind where the legs would be under saddle. This will pre-train the sideways step under saddle.

PRACTICAL APPLICATIONS

Obedient in-hand responses are essential to the success of all practical applications. The horse should be light to stop and go and should be able to stand immobile calmly. The horse should also be able to quicken and slow its step from lead signals. Once the horse is able to demonstrate clear responses to the basic cues for forward, stop, and yield, training routine tasks such as loading onto a trailer and being caught become straightforward.

Making contact with the unhandled horse

It is an interesting reflection on horse training that we "catch" horses while we "call" dogs! And yet a horse that is difficult to catch can be caught, and trained to "come up" to the handler on command, in a number of ways. This is no more difficult than with a dog.

The unhandled horse can be very difficult to catch if it is left in the field for too long without handling. A period of habituation to the presence of humans is often useful before any training occurs. One of the simplest ways is to hand-feed the horse in small but frequent amounts so that it associates the presence of the human with the arrival of food. When the horse shows interest in the arrival of the person it is a good time to begin the advance-retreat process developed by Australian horse trainer Kell Jeffery around 1910.

Jeffery's advance-retreat system was later incorporated into many contemporary and New Age training systems. It is based on the concept of flight distance (a phenomenon first described by zoologist Heini Hediger), referring to the minimum distance at which a predator can approach an animal such as a horse. Advance-retreat works by progressively decreasing that distance. This method of catching animals is also described by Karen Pryor in *Don't Shoot the Dog* as a way of catching alpacas. Although the alpaca trainers used a clicker as a conditioned reinforcer the theory is the same: Reinforce moments when the animal stops running away by turning away yourself. *Stopping the chase is reinforcing*.

> *When the handler is within touching range, he stretches out his hand; if the horse sniffs it, the handler takes a step backward.*

To begin, the handler walks toward the animal and just before it turns and flees, steps back two steps. If the handler gets too close and the horse turns and runs away, the handler continues to walk after it until it stops running (or, in really extreme cases, slows significantly) and then takes two steps backward. The handler should not scare or chase the horse but just walk quietly after it. Gradually this process will diminish the distance between handler and horse, as the horse's failure to flee is reinforced.

When the handler is within touching range, he stretches out his hand; if the horse sniffs it, the handler takes a step backward. The handler should always step back after giving the animal a food morsel (or laying one on the ground if the horse won't accept it from the hand). Soon the horse will start to follow. It pays to take your time over this and it helps to leave the paddock as soon as the animal has had a morsel of food so that, far from feeling threatened, the horse becomes used to moving toward the handler. Make the horse completely used to touch before attempting to place a headcollar or halter on it. This is best achieved in a safe yard. An unhandled horse will generally follow another into a yard.

It is always best to habituate foals early on to the presence and touch of humans. However, because of

Above *If the horse is wary and tries to escape, closing in will make matters worse as the horse will perceive that running away puts distance between the two of you.*

Right *Gradually approach the horse, but if it looks like it's about to step back, step back yourself. Then approach again. You will be progressively decreasing the distance between the two of you.*

the horse's great propensity to learn through negative reinforcement, it is important not to allow the foal (or any horse) to remove the touch of the handler by quickening or swerving away. It is best to touch the animal on the neck or withers first, then remove the touch during moments of immobility, rather than when it moves. In this way it learns that immobility results in the removal of the touch (which will at first be aversive to some horses).

The next step involves placing a halter on the horse and training it to lead forward, and this is most safely achieved in the yard. This should be safe and enclosed so that the horse does not attempt to jump out, and ideally about 6½ yards (6 m) square. If the horse has paired up with another horse with

> ❝ *Why is it that we 'catch' horses yet we train dogs to come on command?* ❞

manageable leading responses it can follow that horse into the yard. When the lead horse has been removed, a halter can be placed on the young horse. It is generally easier at first to use a webbing halter that is buckled on both the nose strap and the poll strap. Place the head strap around the horse's neck and buckle it (not too close to the head as horses are often initially sensitive about having their heads

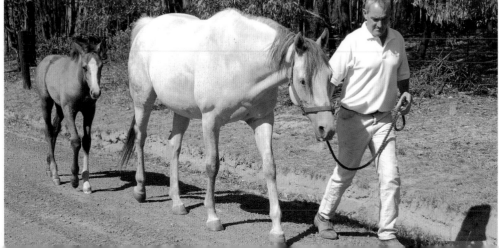

touched). Repeat this frequently to habituate the horse to the strap round its neck, and use wither scratching to promote calmness. Next the nose strap is secured. The horse is now ready to learn the basic responses of forward, stop, and turn.

Training the horse to "come up"

Catching the constantly evasive horse requires it to learn to "come up" on command without hyperreactivity, and training this requires the use of a long whip. It is important that the whip has no unpleasant associations for the horse: If it has been used correctly in training, then it will not be remotely alarming, but if the horse is disturbed, it will need to be habituated to the whip (see p. 77). "Come up" is trained by the use of pressure/release on the hindquarters. The horse learns that when the handler steps to the side, the hindquarters will be tapped with

> *It is always best to habituate foals early on to the presence and touch of humans.*

the long whip until the horse moves them out of sight. This does not result in the horse spinning away every time a human is at its side; it very quickly becomes a context-specific behavior and will occur only in connection with the classically conditioned verbal cue, "Come up."

The handler faces the horse with the lead rope attached to the halter and held quite short. A long whip is held in the right hand. The handler then steps to one side of the horse, focusing on the hindlegs. The handler taps the hindquarters on that side just enough to cause the horse to step away to the other side. The handler is now facing the midline of the horse again. The handler than steps to the other side and immediately taps the hindquarters on that side. This is repeated until the horse anticipates the tapping and steps to the side without it.

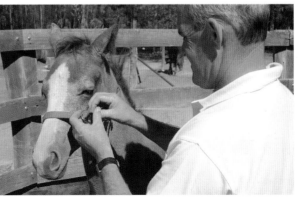

Left *The easy way to catch a foal is to lead it in with the mother, then employ the advance/retreat technique, touching the shoulder first. Stroking the foal and restraining it mildly under the neck prepares it to be secured to the headstall.*

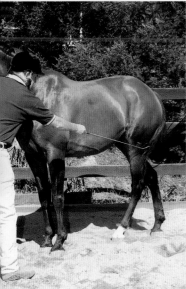  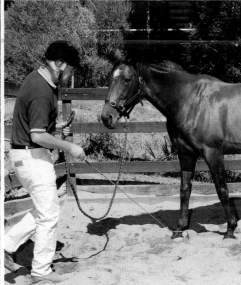 

The horse must not mistake the sideways step for a forward one. If it moves forward it should immediately be stepped back to its original spot. It is important to speed up the footwork so that the horse moves its hindquarters away promptly. One side always moves faster and lines up more clearly with the handler, and it is important to work on that side more than the other.

The lead rope is now lengthened and the sequence repeated. If the handler now takes a step backward just before he steps to the side, the horse will take a step forward toward the handler as well as to the side. When this is occurring relatively reliably

Below *If the horse is overreactive to the whip, habituate it by rubbing the whip all over its body while maintaining the horse's immobility.*

(which should be achieved after a few minutes), the handler can attach a voice command to the behavior, placing it under stimulus control. The handler says the words, "Come up" just as he steps to the side. Over a number of repetitions the words become associated with the response that was originally elicited by the whip tap. It is important to move from one side of the body to the other reasonably quickly, issuing the voice command before every move.

The next step is to remove the lead rope altogether and repeat the above. The horse will continue to follow and move its hindquarters away from the handler's line of sight. The trainer performs more steps backward as well as in an arc toward the horse's hindquarters, and it follows him easily. However, the horse may trial a completely wrong response now that it is free. It may spin away and run to the corner of the yard. At this point the handler should tap his leg or boot with the whip, saying "Come up" just before the tap. The intensity of this behavior is increased until the horse takes a step toward the handler, or at least looks toward the handler. At this moment the handler stops and turns away from the horse, whip lowered. The horse may run a step or two, but if the pressure is not released, will come up to the handler.

It is possible that the horse may regard the yard in which it was trained as the only place associated with this behavior. Once the responses are installed, however, the horse will come up very quickly and follow the handler on command in a new, larger yard.

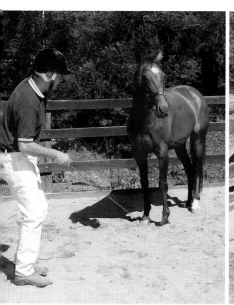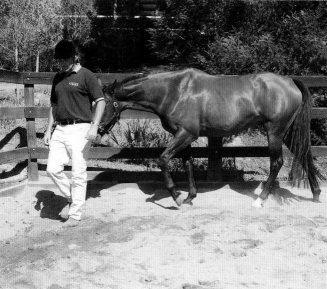

The same may be true when the horse is in the paddock for the first time. It may run for a few steps but very quickly will focus on the handler. The handler again says, "Come up" and walks in an arc toward the horse's hindquarters.

Never just walk up to the horse in these larger yards and paddocks. Always begin by saying "Come up" and, in the absence of a response, walk in a direct arc toward the horse's hindlegs, focusing on them. When the horse moves toward the handler, it is important in the early stages not to move toward it at the same time. After a week or so the horse will have lost its old habit of running away, and should approach when called.

Loading into a trailer

Horses have evolved to be naturally wary of dark, enclosed spaces, so the trailer can be a highly aversive place. Although many never have a problem with loading, some develop an aversion to it very quickly. Because the lead-rope pressure is less aversive to the horse than the trailer, the horse's response to the simple lead pressure needs to be deepened so that it chooses to go into the trailer. This can be done by combining the lead pressure with repeated tapping on the shoulder with the long whip. But take care: The horse must be able to lead well and be habituated to the whip before this is attempted.

Remember the following rules:

- Tap the shoulder with the whip only when you also have the forward direction pressure on the rein.

- Tap with the whip only when the horse is *not* going forward (*never* when it is).
- Increase the intensity of the tapping, but not the lead pressure, when you feel there is no response within a reasonable amount of time.
- Don't leave a pause of more than one second between taps.
- Soften both lead rein *and* cease tapping the very second the horse moves its foot/feet forward.
- Do not miss *any* backward steps with your tapping.

When both tapping and mild head pressure are removed, the horse learns that the pressure of tapping is just another aspect of lead-rope pressure. This deepens its lead-rope response to the point where it is strong enough to overcome any resistance to loading.

It is crucial that the horse is never made uncomfortable when giving the correct response. It is equally important that the pressure is never removed when it is giving the wrong response. It's not a matter of either liking or disliking a trailer; it's all down to having a clear trained response to lead correctly.

Trailer loading is a gradual process of refinement: Begin by training the whole routine with the central partition fully open, then three-quarters open, and so on until the horse offers no resistance. Many people train their horses to load by putting the trailer in a gateway, so the horse can't go past it; but barriers, like gates, are no substitute for training.

To begin the training it is best to have the horse in a thin rope halter—with a rearing bit if the horse

Above, from far left Training the horse to approach on command means first training it to move its hindquarters away to both sides from whip-tap pressure. This evolves to the horse moving its hindquarters to the side as soon as it sees the rider step to the side, even without a lead rope. This evolves to stepping away and to the side. A voice command is added as soon as the horse begins to follow and approach on command.

has a tendency to rear and spin away—to maximize control of its head. In a plain webbing halter it's too easy for the horse to look away from the trailer and perhaps barge off. Take great care of the horse's mouth when using a rearing bit. (I use a rubber-coated one as it is softer.) You should practice stopping the horse with it before issuing corrections. Corrections for rearing and spinning should be given with the lowest level of pressure necessary, and only during the incorrect behavior.

> *If the horse trials rearing to avoid loading, keep tapping until it lands and steps forward.*

The horse must have good leading responses, to both forward and stop cues. If the horse leaps onto the trailer it is using a panic response, and should immediately be stopped from going forward, then the forward cue repeated. Never allow any flight response; it does not lead to quiet loading.

Lead the horse to the base of the ramp and stand facing its rump. This is so if it does run backward the handler can run forward, tapping, to set up an irritation the horse will want to avoid. Many horses run off the ramp in a panic. If this happens, it is again because the horse doesn't respond to the forward cue of the lead rope; if it did, it would stop running the moment it felt the lead pressure at the top of its head. As soon as it begins to run, however explosively, run with it, and keep up mild head pressure and quite fast tapping. Run as far as the horse does, and keep tapping until the horse steps forward—and it will. Take care that it doesn't turn away, too.

If the horse trials rearing to avoid loading, keep tapping until it lands and steps forward. A couple of repetitions will bring about a dramatic change. Don't be afraid that it will hit its head on the roof of the trailer; if your tapping stops when this happens, the horse will learn that this stops the tapping and then its flight response as it shoots backward will reward head tossing. Training the horse to lower its head can help here, and it is possible to buy padded head protectors for this purpose. At any rate the horse will quickly learn to

Above and right *In training and retraining to load on a trailer, the forward lead signal is backed up by whip taps.*

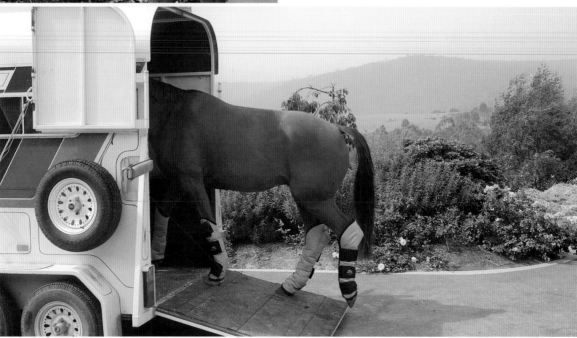

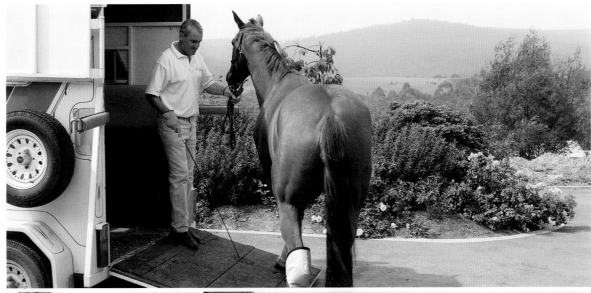

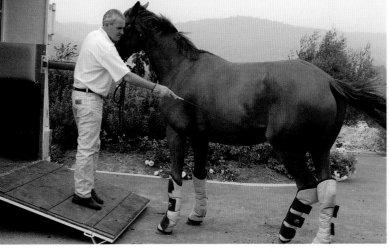

Counterclockwise from left, top *When the horse has a rhythm to go from a light lead signal, issues relating to straightness can be dealt with using the whip on the hindquarters.*

lower its head to avoid the roof. Always remember the fundamental principle of trial-and-error learning: The behavior that precedes the release of pressure is the one that is reinforced. This is the foundation of all basic training: The horse constantly strives after comfort and freedom from pressure.

The aim in loading is to get the horse to step onto the ramp, to take exactly the number of steps asked for, to stop and go back when asked. Spend as much time as you need going back, going forward, and so on: soon you will find the long whip can be discarded. Then make sure the horse focuses on where it is going by maintaining straightness of the head and neck. When a horse doesn't want to go somewhere the first thing it does is look away; to a horse, out of sight really is out of mind. It is also excluding the trainer from its visual picture, which is

" Always remember the principle of trial-and-error learning: The behavior that precedes the pressure is the one that is reinforced. "

quite reinforcing. The next stage is turning away with the shoulders. If it achieves a step in turning away this quickly escalates to the hindquarters and it will attempt to run away; it can all happen very quickly. So it's very important to keep the horse's vision on the task at hand.

If the horse becomes crooked, many handlers will turn away and re-present it at the trailer. Most people think the horse can't load from the side of the tailgate, so they go off on a great big circle to try

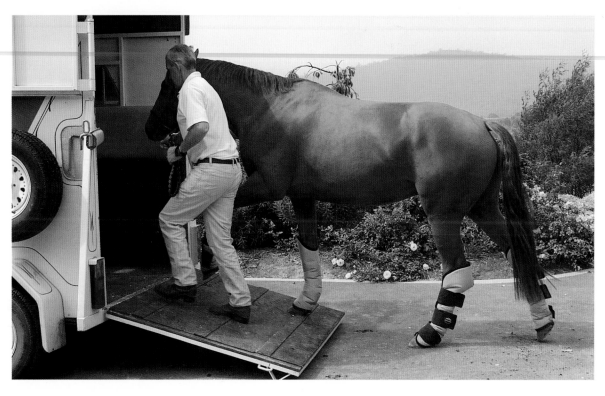

Below *When the horse allows itself to be loaded softly and in a straight line, you can face forward and lead it in normally.*

" *Classical conditioning is not a sufficient basis for a wary horse to enter a trailer.* "

again. This simply trains the horse that turning its neck makes the problem disappear: perfect trial-and-error learning. Horses can load easily from the side, even if they are crooked.

Once the horse is going in smoothly from the side, it is time to straighten its hindquarters. The fact that once a horse has learned to go into the trailer crookedly, it continues to do so highlights just how readily horses form habits and how quickly they become slaves to them. If the horse steps crookedly with its forelegs (usually away from the wall) it should be made to repeat that step at this stage until it steps all the way in a straight line.

Many traveling problems are related to the way the horse leads into the trailer. When people say they have a bad traveler, and I ask if it leads well, they say "Oh yes, it follows me everywhere." But following is not leading. Following the handler into the trailer is fine *if* the horse leads into it as well, but it can be disastrous if it doesn't. It is clear that operant conditioning (trial-and-error learning) must underly classical conditioning. Operant conditioning works

because of its inherent reward: the release from pressure. Classical conditioning (with no such reward) is not a sufficient basis for a wary horse to enter a trailer, and cannot be enforced when things go wrong. At this point leading responses in the horse have to be retrained. Conflicts such as pawing, kicking, and bucking in the trailer (but not scrambling, which is a driving/cornering problem) tend to subside when the horse's leading responses are retrained. Pawing and kicking, for example, are conflict behaviors that arise largely because of random, swerving leg movements in the loading process. They are alleviated by focusing on straightness.

It's a good idea to train horses to walk forward and back all over the ramp, because often horses will walk a particular track and not go on one side of the trailer. The side where they have never set foot becomes a bit of a scary zone. Choose the steps: two steps forward, one step back, one step forward, two steps back, and so on. Also make sure that the horse will stand immobile, anywhere, not because it is being held (the lead rope is loose) but because it's trained and does not move unless a cue has been applied. Reward it with food or scratching at the base of the wither when it is inside the trailer. When the horse is able to load and unload calmly and correctly it is

ready to be "cast" in. This is achieved by leading the horse up the ramp at a constant speed and rhythm and then stopping yourself but encouraging the horse to continue into the box with a mild whip tap on the rump, and tapping faster if the horse tries to back out. This quickly evolves into a habit of self-loading.

Loading into race stalls

This is a similar process to loading a horse into a trailer; it's not difficult, providing the horse has clear training in leading. The young horse should be trained to go forward into difficult places such as over ground with different colors or textures, through puddles, and into shallow ditches. The horse should be trained to go straight rather than swerve at any obstacles that it finds aversive.

Have the front doors of the stalls open at first. The horse is led through (using the same technique as for trailering) a number of times until it walks quietly aand doesn't balk or quicken at all. If it quickens,

gradually stop it closer and closer to the front of the stalls where it emerged. Next it is led into the stalls with the doors held half open, then quietly opened as it moves through. Early on it is too unnerving to have the doors suddenly flung open. The horse should soon walk into the barriers with the doors closed. Although it is tempting to short-circuit this training, it is a mistake to cut corners; if things go wrong in these early stages problems may emerge later. The horse should also be trained (through well-established forward-and-stop responses, rather than food) to stand in the stalls calmly and without moving with all doors open or shut. Panicking, leaping, rearing, and kicking out in the stalls are associated with horses that have poor stop and go responses and will not demonstrate immobility. The horse is now ready to be ridden through using the same shaping process.

Right *First allow the horse to go through the barriers unhindered, then progressively halt it closer to the exit.*

Left and above *Practice immobility in the barriers, then load the horse with the front doors shut, followed by immobility, then finally shut the back doors. Caution—remain in the barriers only if the horse is totally relaxed.*

Holding the horse for the farrier

A well-trained horse makes the farrier's work much easier. However, I sometimes wonder why injuries to farriers are not more common. Generally this is in spite of, rather than because of, the behavior of their client's horse.

Farriers relate stories of how, during bouts of disobedient and dangerous horse behavior, owners reward their horse by soothing and stroking, and seem less concerned for the farrier's safety than their horse's feelings. Sometimes, too, farriers are to blame, for a moment's quick temper can result in a long-term fear association. Farriers should be trained to understand

under control, relaxation and obedience follow automatically. Tension dissipates when it is able to give single clear responses to the go/stop buttons. It is best to have the horse in a bridle or a rearing bit if you cannot control each and every footfall with a halter (and in most cases you can't). Practice your horse's obedience in the places where it is shod; there should be ample clearance from walls, and it should be safe in every way.

The handler stands facing the horse's rump on either the near- or offside (on the same side as the farrier). This means that when the farrier is working, the handler can protect him if the horse suddenly swings its hindlegs and body inward. The lead rope is held with

Above Lowering the horse's head so that the poll is level with the wither makes the horse calmer.

that delayed punishment (and for that matter delayed rewards) are meaningless to the horse. Training quietly is far more effective than endlessly making a ruckus; always remember that you're training, not seeking revenge. When the horse gives incorrect responses, the aim is to get it to behave differently, so certain behaviors are allowed, and others disallowed.

It is the owner's or trainer's responsibility, not the farrier's, to ensure the horse's good shoeing behavior. The aim is to have the horse's feet immobile, its reaction to external stimuli diminished, its body relaxed, loose, and compliant. Once its immobility is

the hand closest to the horse, quite near its chin (3–4 inches [7.5–10 cm] from it), and the thumb closest to its chin. This gives far more control than a long, dangling rope. The handler should wear sensible clothes and footwear, and carry a long whip in the other hand. Finally, especially with young or difficult horses, the handler must be serious about the task at hand; he must not get distracted, or he may miss the vital moments of correction. The aim is to make sure that the handler has fine control of the horse and is able to stop it from moving forward even an inch with the lightest of rein pressure. The jaw should not be involved, and the

neck length should not alter when the horse responds to the lead: The horse should stand immobile in self-carriage.

A horse that is dangerous to shoe will generally have an associated running response or a pattern of stepping forward in some way, so it is imperative to disallow any forward steps. Kicking, a minor expression of the flight response, tends to reduce significantly if there are no associated running steps. If the horse shows any sign of kicking or striking out, the stop response is employed immediately to delete it, strongly and swiftly.

Any loss of straightness in the horse's head and neck can be seen as a precursor of the flight response. The sequence of sideways panic responses starts with the head (focus), then if not corrected spreads to the shoulders (turn away), and if not corrected spreads to the hindquarters (run away). Use light tugs of the bit sideways to correct straightness, away from the direction of turn, offering lightness when the horse gives the correct response. Obedience and calmness are more deeply embedded when the horse cannot exclude the handler from its vision.

Lowering the horse's poll below the line of its withers also deepens calmness: "Head down" is associated with tranquillity. Once any adrenaline is dissipated, the eyes become drowsy, blinking is slower, and the ears become floppy. When the farrier is working the poll needs only to be lower than the wither, otherwise the horse may not be well balanced. Remember to increase pressure quickly if it attempts to raise its head, and be equally quick to soften pressure when it lowers it. The horse's head should go down and stay down, no matter what the farrier does. When the farrier picks the horse's foot up and starts tapping, even when he puts the hot shoe on and it starts smoking, the horse's poll must always remain lower than the wither, and it must be obedient to the light signals of stop and go.

When the farrier (or assistant) picks up the horse's leg, the handler needs to ensure that the leg stays calm

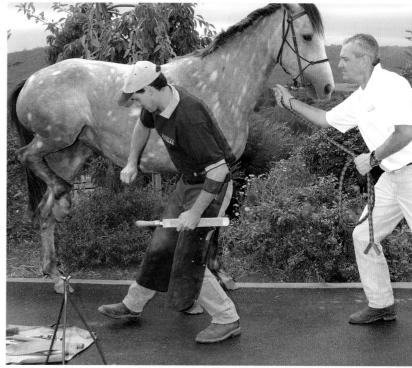

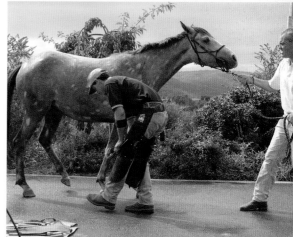

Above and right If the horse kicks free and runs forward, send it back; if it kicks and goes back, pull it forward. Use a pressure appropriate to the resistance, and vibrate the lead during any minor resistances.

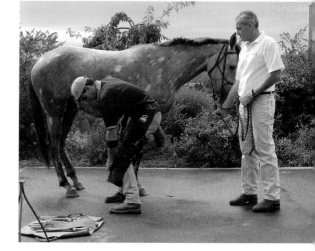

> " *With young or difficult horses, the handler must be serious about the task at hand: He must not get distracted, or he may miss the vital moments of correction.* "

Right *When very
clear in-hand work
is in place, the horse
should be tied to a car
inner tube using a
webbing pull-back
collar slung through
its headcollar.*

> *Every problem behavior that the horse can
> exhibit in hand can be retrained by simply
> reestablishing the basic leading responses.*

and loose, not heavy, rigid, moving, thrashing, or kicking. This is where the bit in the mouth really is useful. The farrier/assistant needs to let the handler know how much tension there is in the horse's leg. The handler then has to exactly match that level of tension with lateral vibrations of the bit in the mouth. These vibrations will negatively reinforce the horse's aversion to maintaining its leg in the farrier's hand. If the horse simply becomes heavy in the farrier's hand, the bit should immediately be vibrated rapidly but reasonably softly side to side at the rate of about five vibrations per second. This must be kept up throughout the duration of the leg tension, and the intensity increased when the horse increases the leg tension. Most importantly, vibrations cease or reduce when the horse stops or lowers the tension. The key is to smother the entire period of resistance with the vibration, and not to vibrate at all when the horse shows calmness.

If the horse shows violent behavior, kicks, or throws its leg to the ground and becomes free of the

farrier, immediately give firm vibrations on the bit to the point where the horse will go immediately backward a step, then ask for another, then another, all in rapid succession. The handler should not make excuses for the horse; this is dangerous behavior and a common cause of injury to farriers. Any behavior that endangers humans is unacceptable. The key is to match the horse's degree of resistance with the degree of discomfort with the sideways vibrations of the bit. When the horse has been trained to stand still, looking

straight ahead with a lowered head position, it will be clear that its relaxed stance has nothing to do with subservience; this is relaxation, free of stress or conflict.

Tying up

Training the horse to be tied up is just an extension of the lead forward response. Pressure felt on top of a horse's head is the same, whether it emanates from its pulling back when tied, or from being led. But a difference may arise when the horse resists: If this occurs while the horse is being led, the trainer can increase the pressure until the horse steps forward. However, when tied to something immoveable the lead rope can break, reinforcing the horse's action of pulling back. Thus it is important to train the horse that these resistances will not be reinforcing.

Although stepping backward might seem irrelevant here, it can highlight poor lead forward responses if the horse is asked to step back then

wall should be safe. Some trainers use a car inner tube. The horse is tethered to this, which in turn is fixed to a wall. The best knot to use is a bowline, and the lead rope should be short (about 30 inches [80 cm] from chin to post). When the horse pulls back, the inner tube acts like a very strong "arm" with increasing pressure, in that its resistance is proportional to the behavioral response of the horse. When the horse is no longer prone to trialing incorrect responses, it is possible to "bag down" the horse with towels and bags—even progressively noisier plastic bags. This is part of the important process of desensitizing the horse to visual and aural stimuli, without its feet moving. The process is finalized when the horse is tied up without the inner tube. The horse should also become accustomed to being tied to other places, preferably with the inner tube at first.

Every problem behavior that the horse can exhibit in hand can be retrained by reestablishing the basic leading responses. It is possible to think of these responses as a simple alphabet that can be rearranged

Left The rope is tied to a car inner tube that is placed over a strong, safe pole. The tube acts like a strong arm, and only gives when the horse steps forward. Always tie horses with a quick-release knot.

forward immediately after. A horse that pulls back will stall and throw its head up during this unexpected forward step. Pressure should be maintained throughout the head toss until the forward step is achieved. This should be repeated until forward steps are occurring quickly without head-tossing.

Every horse needs to be tethered to a solid post or wall at some time. It should never be tied so low that it can get its feet over the rope if it panics, and the post or

to form all the words that the horse ever needs. With a simple alphabet of half a dozen or so letters the horse can be trained to be obedient and calm in every situation. All the responses in hand must therefore be trained to incorporate timing, speed and rhythm, line and straightness, and connection and outline as baselines. Their order is important, as they reflect a gradual refinement of response.

> *"... (The training exercises should) all follow one another in such a way that the preceding exercise always constitutes a secure basis for the next one. Violations of this rule will always exert payment later on; not only by a triple loss of time but very frequently by resistances, which for a long time if not forever interfere with the relationship between horse and rider."*

The Gymnasium of the Horse, Gustav Steinbrecht (1808–1885)

CHAPTER 7
TRAINING UNDER SADDLE

IN THIS CHAPTER I WILL PROVIDE A BLUEPRINT FOR TRAINING UNDER SADDLE. WE WILL DECONSTRUCT TRAINING OUTCOMES TO SINGLE IRREDUCIBLE RESPONSES AND QUALITIES, THEN BUILD RESPONSES ONE BY ONE. THIS WILL ALLOW US TO TAILOR OUR EQUESTRIAN NEEDS MORE PRECISELY TO COMPLEMENT THE HORSE'S PSYCHOLOGY.

We begin with a horse that has learned to lead and respond to the basic in-hand requirements. The training plan we are now going to follow applies equally to young horses and to horses with behavior problems that need to be retrained. Such animals need to be taken back to the foundation training stage—some people refer to this stage as "rebreaking."

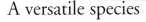

The sorts of behavior problems that indicate the need for retraining are caused by the disintegration of the signal/response mechanism. Many owners of difficult or problem horses don't realize this at first; they believe that the horse mostly goes well because sometimes it wants to and sometimes it doesn't. But when all the horse's movements are broken down into basic responses, and then reduced to irreducible qualities, it becomes clear that so-called "perfect" horses aren't so perfect after all, even when behaving. It also reveals that bad behaviors are caused by training errors.

A versatile species

Recent archeological studies of bit wear on horse's teeth have shown that horse riding began in Kazakstan around 3500 B.C.E. The use of the horse provided an unprecedented advantage in game hunting and then later in war, and this had significant effects on the distribution of various races and cultures of humans throughout much of Eurasia. The first documented horse trainer, Kukkuli, wrote his methods on clay tablets around 1360 B.C.E. These were somehow acquired by the Hittites, who used this knowledge to annihilate Kukkuli's people and culture, and transform themselves into a mighty power rivaling Egypt.

The domestic horse has been selectively bred over a period of 6,000 years. No other species provides the speed, endurance, and comfort of the horse; no other animal can jump obstacles up to 8 feet (over 2 m) high with a human passenger astride. The modern performance horse was developed from four ancestral types: two ponies from Northwest Europe and North Eurasia (cold-adapted), and two horses from Central Asia/Europe and Western Asia (heat-adapted). The type from Western Asia was responsible for the more sensitive, fine-boned characteristics of the Arabian and thus the Thoroughbred.

The origin of equestrian sports

The range of modern equestrian sports reflects the diversity of the ridden horse in recent history. There are equestrian sports that test the physical ability of the

horse, such as endurance riding, where participants cover hundreds of miles; not surprisingly the predominant breed here is the Arabian and various Arab crosses. The individuals that do best are those that resemble human marathon runners: smaller, wiry types with high "heart scores" and low standing heart rates, sometimes below 20 beats per minute (the average is 44 beats). The heart score is an electronic measurement of the size of the heart relative to the body, and the Arabian outsizes all other breeds.

Show jumping tests the heights and widths that horses can jump without error or refusal. Dressage tests obedience and suppleness over many prescribed movements. These evolved from the fast, agile maneuvers required in war. As armory became an advantage in battle, horses were selectively bred to carry the extra weight, and training requirements altered too. Movements became slower, more powerful, as the emphasis changed from sheer speed to power: The horse had to carry most of its weight on its hindquarters, freeing its shoulders for turning relatively quickly.

Horse trials evolved from military tests of the versatile cavalry horse. The horse's obedience and suppleness came under scrutiny—dressage—as did its skill and endurance in cross-country jumping and finally its agility in show jumping, and thus eventing was born. The agility sports of cutting and roping developed from cattle farming in the large open spaces of Australia and the Americas. There are also sports based on "games" for horse and rider that involve speed and agility around barrels and poles.

In Britain and Australia horses were once shown at agricultural shows and judged subjectively on

"Dressage tests obedience and suppleness over many prescribed movements. These evolved from the fast, agile maneuvers required in war."

conformation and ridden work. This has burgeoned into a discipline known as "showing." Nowadays this has little to do with agricultural demands and everything to do with grooming, rider costume, conformation, and training. Possibly the most economically significant area of equine sport is racing, probably the only equestrian enterprise (apart from pleasure riding) that is seen all over the world. Polo, and its derivation polo crosse, are the only truly team ball sports played on horseback.

The horse is also used extensively for pleasure riding. Commercial operations throughout the world cater to trail rides as a form of adventure tourism. It is possible, for example, to ride alongside a migrating herd of wildebeest in Africa, or go on a horseback safari following the old cattlemen's mustering tracks. These rides, covering many days, are probably the most enjoyable and certainly the fastest way to learn to ride in balance. Rodeo and "buck-jumping" events evolved in Australia, Canada, and the Americas, where wild horses are "broken" in a very short span of time. There are great rodeos and festivals based on the extraordinary talents of those who can ride the wildest of horses for eight seconds or so.

In the faster and more agile equestrian disciplines, position and balance skills associated with accelerations, decelerations, and turns are important. Thus, the rodeo sports are dominated by the United States, Australia, New Zealand, and Canada, and those countries (as well as the United Kingdom, with its history of hunting on horseback with hounds) tend to dominate eventing.

The aims of training under saddle

As with in-hand work, training under saddle is all about placing the movements of the horse's legs under stimulus control. The first signals that the horse learns are the primary signals (light versions of the pressures used to elicit them). Later the well-trained horse is influenced by secondary signals: the postural and weight signals (and also the voice to some extent). These signals develop naturally, through the process of classical conditioning ("anticipation").

The trained, "educated" horse does not experience a revelation at some point in its training where it chooses to follow the languid gymnastics of its rider; it must learn clear basic signals of control and develop these into more solid habits. Later these become elicited by the postural mechanics of the rider. Just how amazing is this? Imagine a vehicle controlled totally by the subtlest changes in posture and weight distribution —it is surely the penultimate form of control, second only to controlling something using just the mind!

The effect of the rider's posture

The mode of delivery of the signals to the horse should be consistent. For this reason, riding masters through the ages have concentrated on the position and posture of the rider.

Because the horse is constantly moving not only its legs but also its back and neck, and because these movements differ from gait to gait, training under saddle requires significant balance and position skills. It is not surprising, therefore, that many European systems of equitation require riders to spend hours each day astride a horse on the lunge line to develop position and balance. This reduces the temptation to hold on with the hands, which would detrain the mouth responses of the horse. This system produces a large proportion of the best dressage riders in the world. In the early days of the Olympics, dressage was dominated by those European countries with cavalries.

During early training of the rein signals, when the horse's stop response is heavier and inconsistent, it is important to be sitting upright, not leaning back as many riders do. It is essential that the rider's hands move with the horse in walk and canter, and that there is a straight line from the bit in the horse's mouth to the rider's elbows. There are mountains of books that describe the position of the rider very clearly, so I do not intend to elaborate on this here. Position problems inhibit the development of trained responses in the horse. In general, to train the basic responses, the rider must have sufficient independent balance so as not to rely on the hands and legs, and to ensure that signals are issued consistently. In the training of stop/slow, it is helpful for the rider to slow or cease his seat movements while using the rein aids.

When the horse's training is consolidated, it learns to respond to secondary signals. For example, it will soon stop and slow from the seat alone; it will turn the forelegs left and right by simply sensing a change in the body as the rider turns his shoulders a little to the right (the horse feels this through the seat and the outside leg that comes closer to its side).

Further down the track, fine details of rider mechanics and posture can be honed to achieve greater levels of response from the horse through classical conditioning. But when responses go awry, the basics must be retrained. If the basics are ignored, the horse will lose the "boundaries" that are *only* provided by the pressures of the rein and leg signals, and conflict behavior may creep in. Trainers should assess the depth and qualities of rein and leg responses as part of the warm-up prior to all training.

Preliminary training in hand

Before foundation training under saddle commences, thorough in-hand work is essential. This should be carried out in a bridle (see p. 62). The bridle can be fitted (without reins) and left on the horse for up to an hour to habituate it. Doing in-hand work with the bridle means that the horse has also learned the stop response from the bit—it stops in a uniform way in terms of timing; speed and rhythm; line and straightness; and connection and outline, as described in Chapter 6. The in-hand work has pre-trained the

Left *Habituating the horse to the bit involves leaving the bit in its mouth until the horse's mouth becomes still. Although this is commonly called "mouthing," the term "mouthing" actually refers to the horse learning to stop and turn from the bit.*

"brakes" for under-saddle work. In addition the in-hand training of the turn of the hindlegs pre-trains this same response under saddle making this task far simpler.

The other in-hand training responses should also be well installed to avoid any conflicts or confusions in the horse at the start of ridden work.

Signals and responses

Under saddle, the signals that elicit the various movements of the horse are derived from the rider's hands (via the reins) and legs (squeezing the horse's body). The primary signals or "aids" are as follows:

- GO FORWARD, QUICKEN, or LENGTHEN —pressure from both the rider's legs
- STOP, SLOW, GO BACKWARD, or SHORTEN —pressure from both reins
- TURN FORELEGS RIGHT (TURN)—pressure from the right rein
- TURN FORELEGS LEFT—pressure from the left rein

- TURN HINDQUARTERS RIGHT (YIELD)— pressure from the rider's left leg
- TURN HINDQUARTERS LEFT—pressure from the rider's right leg

To recap, these leg and rein signals develop from pressure/release of pressure. The horse's brain "predicts" the release of pressure that follows the increase in pressure, which in turn follows the light signal. The horse learns that the light signal heralds the release. The responses are "shaped" so that they are elicited uniformly.

Later on these signals may be replaced with other cues, but in order to maintain the horse's calmness and obedience, the pressures and signals must be thoroughly trained to be uniform and virtually unconditional. The following must be avoided:

- achieving no response from a signal
- allowing responses that do not arise from signals
- maintaining pressure when the horse has given the required response
- releasing pressure when the horse has not given the required response
- poor timing (releasing pressure too long after the response)
- pressuring/signaling two or more different responses (go, stop, turn forelegs or hindlegs) simultaneously
- using the same signals for different responses
- training head carriage before the horse's legs are under control
- eliciting qualities of responses without the primary response itself (for example, using the reins for influencing head carriage without slowing the horse; flexing the horse without turning it, and so on)
- allowing any expression of the flight response through moving the legs quickly

A note on traditional beginnings

Work on the lunge
Traditional early training of performance horses frequently involves training the animal to lunge around the trainer on a long line. This must be approached with care: Horses that have had little contact with humans may perceive that they are being chased, and show a degree of hyperreactivity. They may go on to associate fear with human contact, and

Right *When saddled for the first time, young horses may be lunged free to get them used to the saddle. Habituation occurs when the horse disregards the girth.*

this is why many young horses are tense on the lunge. For this reason is it not advisable to lunge such horses unless the trainer is confident of being able to delete any sign of hyperreactivity with downward transitions, that is, slowing to the gait below.

Most trainers ignore tension in young horses during lungeing, but this tension can come back to haunt the handler or rider later on. Lungeing may be useful in checking that there is no buck reflex in the horse after the second saddling (see p. 109), but it is no substitute for effective groundwork (in-hand training). Some reasons given for lungeing the young horse are:

- to give the horse practice in wearing the saddle and habituating to the girth pressure
- to tire the horse (actually pointless in the long-term because the horse just gets fitter)
- with side reins to train the horse to "accept" the bit and go "round" (actually counterproductive because the horse learns that the primary response is "round" rather than stop, so it gets confused)
- to develop the young horse's physique (again incorrect: the horse becomes stronger by carrying the rider correctly and developing the appropriate muscles)

The use of long reins

Driving in long reins is common practice in the Western European approach to starting young horses. It involves using very long reins to steer and stop the horse, while sending it forward with flapping reins on the rump, voice commands, or the long whip. Its use under saddle originates from the training of the horse for harness. Equestrian traditions in other cultures do not follow this practice; their methods are more closely aligned with the systems of "natural horsemanship" and the Jeffery Method, where body contact between horse and human is first developed.

To all intents and purposes, driving the young horse is tantamount to chasing it, and, in the wrong

Right *Driving the young horse can be detrimental from the viewpoint of chasing, as well as shortening the neck and the stride, resulting in tension.*

hands, this can lead to problems that require retraining later. The "driver" is not connected to the horse, and so if the horse moves erratically it receives unintentional signals in its mouth. Furthermore the driven horse cannot see the driver adequately behind, so tends to raise its head, promoting a hyperreactive posture, and frequently looks at the driver through one eye only, thus rendering itself crooked in the head and uneven in rein contact. Driving may also shorten the horse's neck, so it confuses neck shortening with stop/slow. The length of the reins (13 feet [4 m]) and their weight makes a clear release of rein pressure impossible. It is not surprising that the driven horse frequently develops a heavier mouth early on, and a considerable degree of inherent hyperreactivity.

When the horse is trained, and has consolidated responses of clear and calm associations with humans, driving is not detrimental. Many dressage trainers use this technique to train or shape certain movements such as piaffe or passage.

Let's take a look at all the requirements of under-saddle training. Some of the early work involves habituation—familiarizing the horse to various things—and later moves on to operant conditioning (trial-and-error learning) via negative reinforcement to install signal/response connections. Each response must then be shaped through the order of qualities listed for in-hand training in Chapter 6.

A BLUEPRINT FOR UNDER-SADDLE TRAINING

"New Age" training methods demonstrate clearly that there is simply no need to lunge or drive the young horse. Training is made simpler and calmer for the horse if the handler focuses on clear in-hand work, then approaches the task of foundation training as one of habituation to the following visual and aural stimuli:

- the human during all aspects of mounting the horse, including sitting astride
- the saddle, girth, and other gear

Habituating horse to rider bareback

This is an important part of creating a relaxed horse-human bond. The establishment of this contact is maintained by preventing the horse from moving its feet during the habituation process. We noted earlier how the Blackfoot Indians of North America sometimes rode their horses for the first time in boggy ground or chest-deep water. Some breakers today use hobbles (tethering one leg to the other) or leg ties (tying the foot to the upper leg through bending the knee) to restrict the movement of the horse's legs. But this is unnecessarily harsh.

It is both safer and more ethical to effect this immobility via the trained stop response in hand, supported by both the Jeffery Method and the Parelli System. These promote mounting the horse bareback during early foundation training. The body-to-body contact is most important in establishing horse/human habituation.

The horse needs to be progressively habituated to all aspects of mounting, as well as sitting astride. The rider must maintain light contact with the reins in the left hand as he mounts from the left side of the horse so that he can stop the horse from moving forward. Every time the horse moves forward, the process of habituation to the rider is prevented, so it is essential to disallow forward or sideways movement. If the horse moves backward, however, this does not constitute an expression of the flight

> *Rushing things will result in an overload of neural pathways, leading to conflict.*

- jumping up and down beside the horse but not touching its body
- jumping up and down beside the horse and contacting its body
- jumping up and lying briefly across its withers, before jumping off immediately
- jumping up and lying across its withers
- lying across its withers and stroking the horse with the right hand on its right side
- lying across and bringing the right knee gently over the horse's spine
- lying across and bringing the lower right leg across its spine to its right-hand-side rump
- scratching and caressing the horse's rump with the

response, and the horse will stop of its own accord (the rider is powerless to prevent backward movement as the forward signal is not yet trained).

The habituation of horse to rider astride involves 12 separate features that must be reduced to single steps. Each step is repeated until the horse lowers its head in relaxation, at which point the next step is attempted. These single steps are as follows:

1 *The first stage is jumping up and down beside the horse. Care must be taken to ensure a light connection to the horse's mouth.*

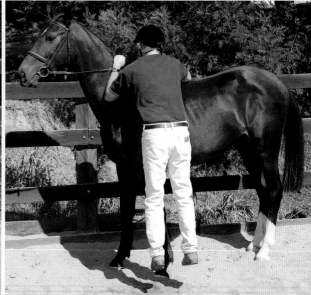

2 *At every step the horse habituates to the rider, and the rider gauges when to move to the next stage by the horse's head carriage (high or low).*

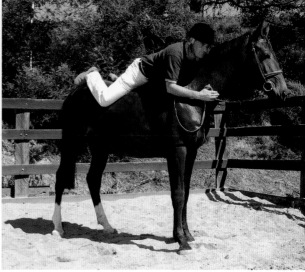

right foot as you lie prostrate along its back
- bringing your legs to the horse's sides
- gently rubbing your legs along the horse's sides
- sitting up a little, then lowering the body, sitting up a little further, then lowering, and so on
- sitting up and caressing the horse at the base of the withers and then all around the neck area

Each step is repeated and no advance made until the horse has habituated to the previous one. The aim is for the horse to maintain a low head posture throughout the 12 steps: This is a sign that it is relaxed and is ready to move on to the next stage. If tension arises, simply go back a step or two. When the habituation process is complete, the horse will be relaxed when the rider sits up.

It is now time to train the horse to respond to leg and rein signals. The saddle can be introduced at this stage, or it can be done bareback. I like to achieve a basic go, stop, and turn response before I introduce the saddle. This way the horse is familiar with some controls when it is first ridden under saddle. It doesn't matter how long foundation training takes: the longer, the better. Take your time, and thoroughly habituate and train the horse in every step. Rushing things will result in an overload of neural pathways, leading to conflict.

Training the basic responses

Once the horse has habituated to all aspects of the mounting process bareback, work begins in earnest with the training of the "basic attempt" of go, stop, and turn the forequarters.

At first glance, it makes sense to train "go" first. But the problem with initiating go from halt for the first time is that increasing pressure from the rider's legs is likely to initiate a random response, because the horse doesn't know how to react. To avoid the risk of a hyperreactive response, which could be difficult to control or even dangerous, some trainers lead the naïve horse for the first time on foot or on horseback. The rider gradually introduces the go signal just as the leader/lead horse moves off, and so the horse learns the beginnings of the signal. This very basic go signal can now be shaped by negative reinforcement.

I don't use a lead horse or person. Instead I signal the horse bareback to perform a single step of turn of the forequarters by vibrating the turning rein with increasing frequency until it performs the step. When pressuring the turn step for the first few times sufficient pressure should be applied to the opposite side rein because of the horse's tendency to bend its neck before (or instead of) turning the legs: The outside rein helps keep the neck straight and propels the horse to turn.

In bareback bonding, it is important to use the reins to prevent any forward or sideways movement.

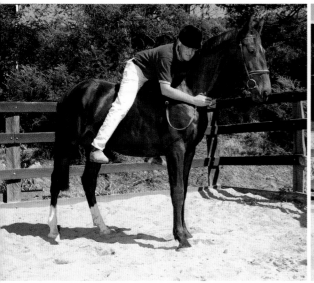

1 *The turn step is the first to be initiated. The turn rein is vibrated until the horse steps over.*

2 *Soon the horse is turning more softly.*

3 *If the horse attempts to rush, it is slowed with the reins.*

If it does not respond I dismount and train the turn step standing beside the horse, my hands on either side of its neck and pushing its shoulder with my hip. I repeat this until the turn is easy. Then I remount and try again bareback. When the horse is capable of turning to one side or the other from the single-rein pressure (released the instant the horse completes one step), the rider nudges with both legs at the end of the turn step to transform the action into forward.

If the trainer is adept in the timing of pressure/release, the forward step that is pressured during the turn quickly results in the horse learning the go signal. It generally takes only five or so repetitions for the horse to have learned to go forward from the pressure of both legs. In later sessions the horse may forget the go signal and the turn may need to be reutilized, but usually the horse will already have a go response. When the basic attempt of go is installed but the horse is losing forward, clucking with the tongue can be used to raise the horse's alertness as it is pressured with the legs. This should be discontinued as soon as possible so it does not overshadow the leg signal.

4 *Soon the horse is pressured to offer more steps forward from the turn—until it can go from stop to forward.*

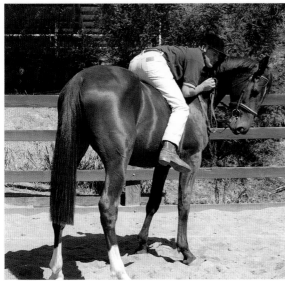

Now it is time to remind the horse of its stop response, learned in hand. While the horse is walking, apply an even rein pressure, increasing it until the horse stops its legs, and releasing the pressure as it does so.

The importance of rein connection

During early foundation training it is critical that the horse is ridden in the "natural outline"—the neck is allowed to be the length that the horse chooses. As the

trainer goes through the qualities of the responses, he notices that the outline becomes naturally rounder. The neck-and-head position is the barometer of good training. It is important not to force it. Otherwise, confusion and hyperreactive responses will emerge. The connection of the rider's hands to the horse's mouth is merely a gossamer-light feel of the lips and tongue—just enough pressure to keep the rein straight. Any greater pressure and the horse is likely to stop (which, via the learned responses in hand, would be a correct response).

Consolidating pressure release

At this stage the horse is still largely a "blank slate": It has no established responses to the ridden signals, so it learns these very rapidly indeed. As long as the amount of pressure is just enough to motivate the horse to produce a response, and the release is timed precisely for when it gives the correct response, it can learn the go and stop signals in as few as five repetitions. It will not at this stage have reliable habits, but the response is gradually becoming attached to the signal. At first the responses are dull, but they rapidly improve so that by the fifth attempt the horse is virtually responding to the light versions of the respective signals.

If the horse has good habits in early training it will fall back on these in times of conflict. However, if it has confusion early on, it has no backup. *The most important maxim in training is that pressure motivates, and release trains.*

Within a single half-hour session on the first day of training the signals correctly, the horse responds more softly and thoroughly to lighter signals than most horses that have been ridden for years. Many horses suffer a considerable level of "detraining" because riders are not aware of the correct application of pressure release.

When the horse is developing the beginnings of a clear learned response, it may emit a long snort. This shows that it is breathing easily. The horse may even shake its neck slowly, or lick its lips; these are all signs of relaxation, and indicate that a clear response is emerging from the signal. This training of the signals for go and turn, and the reminding of the stop response bareback, should be repeated for three or so sets of five improved or correct responses daily for three or four days.

Above left Alternatively, the first steps may be achieved by leading the horse with the rider astride; as the horse steps, the rider squeezes/nudges its sides. Left At all bareback stages, it is good to retrace your steps, rubbing, scratching, and caressing the horse as often as possible. A soothing voice is soon associated with this.

Left *Before saddling it is a good idea to allow the horse time to sniff the saddle pad.*

> *When the horse is reliable from day to day with bareback work, the saddle is introduced.*

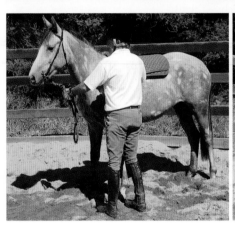

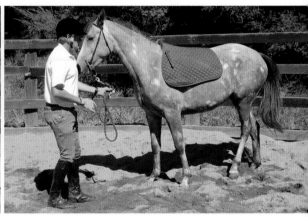

Above right *After the horse has sniffed the saddle pad, rub the pad on the horse and place it in position. To speed up habituation, signal a step back.*

I have broken in thousands of horses and have been bucked off bareback only three times. Each time it was because I didn't look for the signs of relaxation before I moved on to the next step. When the horse is reliable from day to day with bareback work, the saddle is introduced.

Habituating horse to saddle

First the horse must be habituated to the saddlecloth, again through restricting its movements with the stop response in hand.

The saddle pad is calmly brought toward the horse, and taken away again, until the horse shows no reaction and has habituated to the extent that placing the cloth on its back does not cause it to raise its head. The horse is habituated to the sight of the saddle in the same way, and should then be habituated to the repeated contact of the girth strap around its rib cage until it shows no reaction and maintains its low head carriage.

When the horse is habituated to the feel of the girth, the next step is to tighten it. Although it may seem ideal to do this progressively, the problem is that if the girth is too loose and the horse shows an intense hyperreactive response such as bucking, the saddle may slip around, resulting in a dangerous situation. This is a response to the ultimate predatory assault: Switch off all sensitivity to the otherwise subduing effects of pain and simply run and buck.

Carefully restrain the horse by the lead rope and tighten the girth sufficiently to prevent any slipping. If reins are attached to the bridle they are safely looped and fastened around its neck. The horse may then be released inside the safe, high-fenced yard. Some horses buck at this stage and the handler should step back on release, as occasionally a horse can leap forward immediately and inadvertently kick out to the side. The degree of hyperreactivity varies from horse to horse: Sometimes the quietest of horses buck violently, while others you might expect to do so remain calm. Most horses don't buck, but it is safe procedure to leave them on their own in the yard during this stage.

There are two diverging opinions concerning this early girthing process. Some trainers like to let the horse run free to buck in the hope of rapidly habituating it to the girth: The horse discovers the futility of trying to buck the girth pressure off. The other way is to prevent the horse from bucking by restraining it and using strong stop pressures in hand or on the lunge when it does so. The rationale behind this thinking is that if the horse never practices this type of fear response then a future repeat is less likely. This approach seems to have merit, given how rapidly hyperreactive survival responses are learned: Sometimes

only two or three repetitions are required to confirm behavior such as bucking, rearing, and shying. But allowing the horse to buck just once on the first occasion makes little difference to the likelihood of reproducing the response at some later time.

When the horse has trialed its saddle buck (or had it thwarted), the trainer lunges it again, but must immediately stop or slow the horse's legs if it displays any hyperreactive responses. This is achieved by tugging the rein as strongly as necessary to achieve the slowing/stopping response. The horse will then lunge quietly. After a number of transitions from halt to walk and walk to halt, transitions to trot and even canter should be attempted. This is repeated later

Below The saddle is introduced as before and quietly placed on the horse's back. The horse maintains immobility through the rein contact during girthing up. The reins are unclipped and the horse is released.

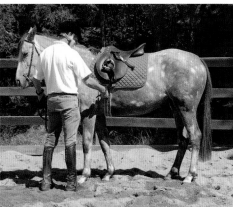

Below Some horses, especially those sensitive in the girth area, buck when first girthed. One bout of bucking has no long-term negative effect; however, the second time around the horse should be stopped.

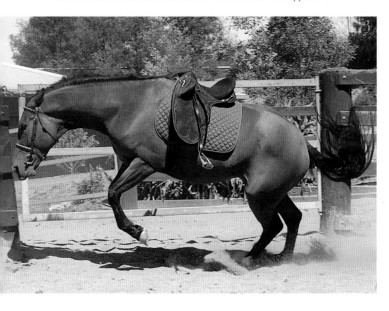

Above The second time the horse is saddled, it should be on a lunge line so bucks can be deleted with a tug of the lunge line.

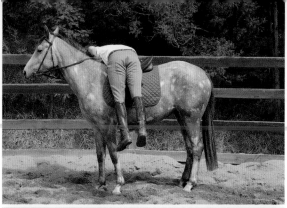

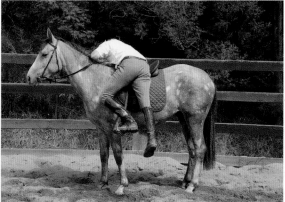

Above *Second time around, any bucking is deleted with sufficient downward vibrations on the lunge rein to slow the horse. The vibrations should be mild but may cause the horse to raise its head.*

Above *Lungeing can be continued provided the horse is calm. This deepens habituation to the saddle, which may flap a little during motion. Any quickening is slowed.*

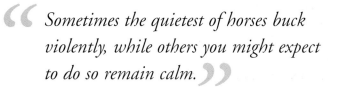

Sometimes the quietest of horses buck violently, while others you might expect to do so remain calm.

Above *Following saddle habituation the rider mounts the horse, placing the foot in the stirrup when already leaning over the horse. Caressing the neck deepens relaxation.*

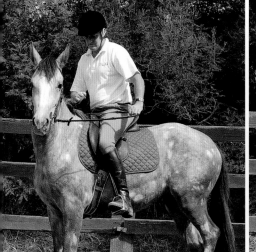

Left *As with bareback work, the first go forward steps under saddle are derived from the turn.*

with stirrups slightly lowered to habituate the horse to these flailing around the shoulders and ribs, so as to prepare it for similar circumstances later in life, such as when the rider falls off, loses the reins, and the horse runs free.

Mounting with the saddle

As the horse has not been habituated to being mounted by someone using stirrups, this is done in the same way as mounting bareback, by jumping up. Providing the horse has been thoroughly habituated to the saddle, the girth, and the rider on board, it will remain calm. After a few repetitions, the rider can begin to mount in the usual way, by placing the left foot in the left stirrup. This puts a considerable strain on the girth and saddle, and therefore on the horse's rib cage, and the rider should aim to keep his body mass as close as possible to the horse to alleviate sideways pressure on the horse's back. The rider must begin with only mild pressure on the stirrup and spring up onto the horse. The amount of spring can be reduced as the horse, with practice, habituates to the strain.

Shaping the basic responses

We are now ready to begin to shape the basic responses through the qualities, just as we did in hand in Chapter 6. In a retraining situation the qualities are

trained in the same order, and here it is particularly important to begin at walk. Practically all problems show up in the walk. In the trot they are magnified, and in the canter they are generally super-magnified. Training at walk tackles the problem at its root.

It is vital to understand that all problems—in timing, rhythm, straightness, or connection and outline—boil down to a question of speed: The horse either slows, quickens, or offers no response. Retraining problem areas is therefore a matter of reinstalling stop and go responses under stimulus control.

1 Basic attempt

The "Basic attempt" of go, stop, and turn refers to the horse giving a "crude" response: that is, going forward, regardless of quality. At this stage the horse will require plenty of rest periods within each training session as the neural pathways that connect the stimuli to the responses develop.

Under saddle, the basic response of go can be more subtly produced by hijacking a turn as described earlier if the horse has forgotten the go response from the signal. This largely depends on the quality of the bareback work. To train the turn of the forelegs, a single step from both forelegs is the correct response.

Training the basic responses is the first stage in a long process of shaping. It is similar to making a sculpture: The first part involves hacking a large slab of stone to produce a rough outline. The "Basic attempt" is similar. It doesn't matter how the horse goes forward or stops or turns, just that it does so from the correct signal. The transitions are repeated so that this crude response becomes reliable.

In the training of go, the rider should target only a quiet, albeit crude go: that is, a movement of the legs in a forward direction, no matter how ungainly. Excessively hyperreactive steps are deleted with downward transitions that are followed by the upward ones to ask for the response again until calmer steps arise. Training go and stop is about training on straight lines. The turns of the forelegs are

Below The horse is pressured with the nudging legs of the rider to take faster steps. These soon become longer, and the horse relaxes and lowers its head.

trained to the level of connection and outline. The turn of the hindquarters must be elicited from the rider's *single leg* only, whereas the *single rein* elicits the turn of the forelegs. Training of the turn of the hindquarters evolves into what dressage trainers call "leg-yielding" and what Western trainers refer to as "side-passing."

2 Timing

Now that the horse has been trained to produce the roughly correct response, the trainer focuses on the "timing" of the responses. Pressure is sufficiently intensified after the light aid to ensure that the responses of go, stop, and turns are initiated immediately, elicited by light versions of the signals

> *Excessively hyperreactive steps are deleted with downward transitions that are followed by the upward ones...until calmer steps arise.*

about training turns and circles. Go and stop should be trained on straight lines because circles, no matter how large, are a development of turns, which need specific training.

The turn of the forelegs is ideally trained after speed and rhythm of stop and go are relatively reliable. The turn of the hindlegs can interfere with the turn of the forelegs, and should not be trained until stop, go, and turn of the forelegs are thoroughly

within three beats of the rhythm. This is achieved through increasing the pressure of the signal and releasing the pressure precisely when the horse offers the desired response. Thus the responses begin to emerge in three beats of the rhythm of the gait. This is the stage where *the horse learns that the light aid "tells" it what the rider is about to do, the pressure motivates it to do it immediately, and the release trains it to actually do it*—and the horse ends up relieving itself of the stronger pressure altogether by responding to the light signal only.

The timing of the turn of the forelegs can be trained along a "wiggly" track. This enables the rider to space repeated turns close together. The horse is pressured to turn one way, beginning with the light signal, then the stronger pressure, which is increased

Below *The horse learns to stop from a light rein signal when release rapidly follows the use of pressure. Then, pressure can shrink rapidly to light cues. Caressing induces further relaxation.*

Left *In both foundation training and retraining, when the horse stops from light pressure, the head carriage tends to become consistent.*

Below and right *Horses are naturally inclined to bend their neck as a first response from turn pressure. Maintaining the outside rein flat against the horse's neck prevents this.*

rapidly so that the horse gives the turn response with both forelegs. As the horse turns both forelegs, pressure of the turning rein is released. The hindlegs are pushed forward to complete the turn of all four legs. After a step or so (during which the horse continues without interference) the opposite turn is elicited with the opposite turning rein. Then the horse is signaled again in the original direction, and so on. If the turn is delayed or heavy, increased pressure may be applied via a stronger vibratory tug after the light signal. In only a couple of wiggly lines, most horses, even those with ingrained timing problems, tend to execute more correct turns easily.

Once the horse can turn with good timing, the turn signal becomes classically conditioned and the horse responds to the light signal alone. The turns are now light to the feel—the horse has "power steering"—and the horse is ready to do full circles.

From now on the correctly trained horse should hardly ever require stronger pressures, except perhaps in new and aversive situations, such as going into water or over ditches for the first time. However, providing the horse's training is thorough, even testing environments will not require much stronger pressure. If the workings of negative reinforcement are clearly understood and applied, only minor pressure changes are required. When people experience that this is not so, it is inevitably because the timing of pressures are at fault. Good timing makes the horse's responses sharper and will give it "brightness" in its action. A lack of timing renders the horse dull.

In correct foundation training, the horse learns the responses up to timing level very rapidly, and these are consolidated after only a few sets of repetitions. It can now be turned out to pasture for months, or even years, while still retaining much of its training up to this level.

3 Speed and rhythm

When the timing of go, stop, and turn responses is in place, the trainer may notice that the horse has an element of "cruise control." For go and stop this means that the horse maintains its rhythm by itself.

1 The horse is turning to the right correctly but it lacks "bend"; this is added later in training, at connection and outline level.

2 The horse is signaled with the turn rein to turn left as the left foreleg is leaving the ground.

3 The horse is now turning left with the right foreleg as well.

Rhythm is a critical aspect of training. While all trained horses should have this characteristic, many horses quicken when the reins are released, or slow when the legs are released. Self-maintained speed and rhythm is a major component of what is sometimes called "balance," an aspect of self-carriage that is not always trained to be truly present, and thus a major source of conflict behavior. Self-carriage also requires the horse to maintain its own line and straightness, and connection and outline, but it all begins with speed and rhythm.

From eventing to racing to dressage, riders should be able to let go of the reins without the horse quickening. Lack of self-carriage is why so many cross-country horses, described merely as "bold and eager," are ridden in severe bits. Such horses obviously lose their timing—their responses become very heavy. It is highly confusing for the horse if the stimulus for go is the release of the reins, or the stimulus for slow is the release of the rider's legs. So it is important to test regularly for self-carriage by releasing the reins or legs for only a couple of strides to check that nothing changes.

4 *The horse learns to move its hindquarters over from the pressure of the rider's single leg.*

For the turns, both forequarters and hindquarters, it means that the horse keeps turning/yielding from the light signals. For all responses it means that the transitions are smooth and in three beats.

When rhythm is not present the horse may be obedient to light pressures, but may move his legs too slowly or too fast. In this case the horse must be trained using pressure/release to quicken and slow from leg and rein signals in the three body lengths. These provide a template for training the half-halt, and for correcting straightness and outline problems. When trained they can be incorporated into improving upward and downward transitions if the horse moves his legs too fast or too slow. Training the legs to give the required speed produces what is known as "activity" or "impulsion."

It is at this stage also that the rider's seat, following the movements of the horse's back, begins to have an influence on the rhythm of the horse.

4 Line and straightness

Now that the horse is maintaining its speed, the next major aspect that requires attention is direction and drift. While the horse is traveling, it may be drifting one way or the other. Young horses generally display this tendency during training; it also shows up when the horse makes corners or circles larger or smaller, often without being signaled to do so by the rider. Riders who sit unbalanced in the saddle are often to blame for this: Leaning to one side or the other predisposes horses to loss of line and straightness.

When a horse it not straight it is because it is either quickening or slowing its legs more on one side of the body than on the other. On straight lines this feels like the horse is drifting; on circles and in turns, it feels like the horse is collapsing in or out. These losses of line are shaped or trained using quickening and slowing signals, which later refine to half-halts. Riders can use differential rein pressures (that is, where one signal is stronger than the other) to effect these downward transitions, and differential leg pressures to effect upward transitions in order to regain line. The corrections must be achieved by using primary signals. When the horse slows and bulges its rib cage, the rider makes the horse quicken on the bulging (slowing) side, then slows it with appropriate rein pressures that bring it back onto the original line. Conversely, if the horse quickens and drifts, the rider slows it, again bringing it back into line with the reins. The neck should always be kept straight when slowing, with the rein against the neck on the bulging side. The training of line and straightness in stop and go should be on straight lines, and not against a wall.

Drifting of the forelegs may escalate over time into hyperreactive versions (shying, which, if left unchecked, can develop into running away). For the horse's mental well-being and learning efficiency,

Right *Although the horse is showing adequate speed and rhythm with its legs, its neck is short and its poll is lowered. This causes it to lose speed because the foreleg touches the ground too early compared to the hindleg.*

Here the horse is "falling in" on a lefthand curve. It consequently loses flexibility in bending its neck to the inside, and leans its shoulder to the left.

> *Good timing makes the horse's responses sharper and will give it 'brightness' in its action. A lack of timing renders the horse dull.*

1 In "falling out" the horse has a bent neck and the inside foreleg is disempowered.

foreleg and hindleg corrections should not be made simultaneously.

This stage concludes the basic training for horses in many activities—leisure riding, stock horses, games, polo, and working cow horses (where head and neck placement is largely irrelevant). All these horses now require is consolidation of the responses in various environments—"proof."

5 Connection and outline

When the horse responds with timing and rhythm, and goes straight, the training of the *legs* in go and stop is almost complete. In the sport of dressage, however, the rider also needs to gain control of the horse's *head and neck* carriage, and its connection with the reins and the rider's legs.

Connection and outline refer to the horse's constant and even connection (or contact) with the reins and rider's legs, and the maintenance of a consistent head and neck position, neither tense and high (indicating hyperreactivity) nor too low (indicating stalling and lack of forward). Connection and outline are highly interdependent: Poor connection results in poor outline (high head and neck equals hollow back) and vice versa.

2 To correct falling out the shoulders are brought back on line (turn signal plus straightening the neck with the outside rein). Then, the bulging rib cage is pressured with the outside leg.

Once go and stop responses are correct, relaxation and longitudinal flexion will follow. Longitudinal flexion (a relaxed long outline) should be offered by the horse, not forced by the rider, but is effected through transitions. It should be evident as the rider warms up the horse each day. If a horse has a poor stop or go it is unlikely to exhibit longitudinal flexion.

In the horse's natural life a high head carriage is associated with raised flight response levels and hyperreactivity. When danger threatens, heads are raised. Conversely, a low head carriage is associated with calmness: dozing, grazing, suckling, and so on. Lowering the horse's head in both groundwork and under-saddle work therefore calms it by association. However, if the horse carries its head too low—lower than its withers—it is generally a sign that it is losing speed.

Changes in connection and outline are usually associated with subtle speed changes. If the altered outline is associated with slowing, upward transitions are used to a faster speed or to the gait above. If it is associated with quickening, downward transitions (slowing, or to the next gait if persistent) are used. The transitions are repeated until the horse maintains its speed and rhythm. In cases where there is a connection or outline change but no change in speed, downward transitions are used. With persistently high head-carriage problems stronger rein pressure may be required during the downward transition.

Remember that behavior practiced is behavior repeated, so the transitions should occur as soon as an incorrect step occurs. Thus using rein pressure to lower the outline should occur only during a downward transition; using the reins to do this when *not* doing a downward transition destroys the signal/response relationship between the two. The outline must never be forced with hands or gadgets. During downward transitions the rider must avoid any nose lengthening or contact increases by maintaining hand position and not letting the horse take the reins away.

Right *The correct outline is for the last three vertebrae, including the poll, to be at the highest point, and the nose in front of the vertical face line.*

Many trainers (especially those involved with showing and dressage) get connection and outline wrong: They train the outline (head and neck placement) before the legs are under control. This has been an increasingly damaging trend. Even more detrimental is the fact that too many riders attempt to produce this outline from their hands, without any associated downward transition, and thus the horse is confused because the reins are now a cue for something other than stop or turn. With such a range of responses now arising from a single signal the horse is bound to get tense. With correct training, head carriage becomes an indication of the clarity of the horse's leg responses to signals.

The connection between horse and rider during turns of the forelegs also develops so that the horse exhibits what is known as "lateral flexion" of the head (a particular requirement of dressage). This concerns balance: The horse should turn its head so that the face plane is perpendicular to the line of the circle traveled. The head also lowers a little more as the joint between the neck and head becomes more flexible to the reins. Lateral flexion develops in association with turns when the horse is straight and maintains an even contact on both reins.

The smaller the circle, the greater the lateral flexion. When this is trained, it soon becomes habitual on turning. In early training, therefore, flexion should only be elicited when the horse is turning. The horse also should not be counterflexed while turning (a training technique where the horse is flexed to the

outside of the circle). This detrains the turn and is a source of conflict.

Lateral flexion first appears at the level of connection and outline and further deepens relaxation, producing what is known in dressage as looseness: The horse looks free, regardless of the fact that it has a rider on its back; it moves fluidly, in perfect rhythm, and even to the unaccustomed eye looks like "poetry in motion." The only thing the movement lacks is power, the slight lowering of the hindquarters. That begins to emerge in the next quality of the go and stop responses, adjustability.

When the turns of the hindlegs are trained to the level of connection and outline the horse cruises effortlessly forward and sideways along a diagonal track. Because it has achieved all the earlier qualities it shows its relaxation through a softening of its entire

Above The horse changes speed (of the body) and rhythm (of the legs) when it shortens its neck down or up, or becomes crooked in the neck.

> *The training of all the qualities of the responses results in all of the horse's body becoming equally relaxed, from the poll to the rib cage.*

Above *The connection and outline are stable.* **Right** *The horse is on the rider's chosen line and is straight. Again, the slightly shorter neck has lowered the poll. Straightness is best developed away from the wall.*

body. It appears rounder through the softening of its neck, and its rib cage feels softer under the rider's leg. When the horse is ridden on a circle, its rib cage now softens under the rider's inside leg and it "bends."

The rider is now able to effect turns of the hindlegs with ease, and the development of "bend" completes the process of relaxation of the entire body of the horse. "Bend" adds a further dimension of relaxation to looseness, and this is known in dressage as "suppleness." The horse now looks even more lithe.

"Bend" used to be thought of as a bending of the spine (like a cat), but we now know that this is anatomically impossible in a horse. The feeling of bend occurs because the rib cage and belly of the horse now swing to the side that the single leg is applied on. This allows the same side hindleg to step forward more freely, unhindered by the abdomen of the horse. Thus, bend is important in maintaining the forward response on circles and turns. It allows the hindlegs to follow the track of the forelegs exactly— difficult on tighter circles and more difficult still if the rib cage is stiff and unyielding. Riders can use bend to assist in the carrying of weight on the hindquarters, and to engage the horse so it provides increased power.

The horse now requires time—maybe months—to consolidate training to this level.

6 Adjustability

Now that the rider has complete control of the speed of the horse's legs, head, neck, and body, the only aspect of mobility to be trained is the adjustment of stride length—a requirement in dressage.

Until now, the working paces result in the horse's hindlegs stepping into the prints of its forelegs. Now it needs to be able to step longer and shorter. The horse already has the beginnings of this in the slower and faster steps first trained at speed and rhythm stage. Faster steps naturally evolve to longer steps, and slower

Clockwise from far left
When the basic responses have been consolidated, advanced work, which involves training movements that consist of two or more responses (such as go and turn), can begin. These movements also require training through the seven qualities or basic responses (see p.65). Here extended trot, shoulder in, and half pass are trained.

> ❝ *When the horses' body is fully relaxed and uniformly responsive to the signals, it provides power at the press of the signal.* ❞

increases its activity (speed) as it lengthens without altering the rhythm of its legs.

Redistributing weight to the hindquarters allows the horse to move with a powerful, slow, relatively high-stepping action (collected movements) and to perform lateral movements, the flying change, piaffe, passage, and the canter pirouette. When the horse performs these when not in a collected gait, it is heavy on the forequarters, labored, and cumbersome.

Rein signals are primarily used to elicit shorter strides, and leg signals to elicit longer strides. At this stage, the horse may have learned that the seat accompanies the rein signals, and other subtleties of the rider's position accompany the leg signals. The rider should use the reins and legs to train adjustability to hasten the learning and lower the randomness of responses. At this stage the half-halt is trained.

Timing, speed, line, and contact may all deteriorate to some extent at first, so the training of

steps to shorter ones. Subtle variations in strength of the light rein and leg signals precede the shorter and longer strides. From these beginnings the horse learns the medium and extended paces, as well as the shorter- and higher-stepping collected paces. However, in dressage the real advantage of training in adjustability is that it makes the horse more powerful (called "engagement"). This is particularly true if the horse adjustability requires the qualities of the responses to be progressively reshaped. The transitions from shorter strides to longer strides in dressage typically involve transitions from working or collected strides to medium or extended strides. Signals from the rider's legs initiate activity, and these are followed by a second signal to produce lengthening. Similarly in downward transitions, initial signals result in slowing, followed by shortening of the stride.

The quality of adjustability is the precursor to what dressage trainers refer to as "engagement." The springing of the horse into a lengthened trot, or the "sitting" of the horse in the downward transition, initiates it for later work in dressage where more time is spent carrying weight on the hindquarters. If the horse cannot respond to the rider's signal for longer or shorter strides in three beats of the rhythm, the quest for engagement is doomed.

The horse that is more adjustable can be signaled to turn tighter corners and perform smaller circles with longer strides. Similarly, leg-yielding can be performed on steeper angles, and the horse's legs will begin to cross at hock/knee level.

At this stage the half-halt can be trained. The half-halt is an almost simultaneous use of seat, rein, and leg signals. It becomes a major toll in dressage where it develops collection and engagement, and assists in the development of straightness, connection, and outline. The training of the half-halt itself goes through the developmental stages of the qualities. The rein and seat immediately slow the legs, lowering the hindquarters and making the horse "sit," while the leg signal elevates the horse's stride, producing "springiness."

7 Proof

Many things can affect the quality of the horse's responses from day to day: mistakes during training, genetic predispositions, interactions with other horses and humans, rising planes of nutrition, hormonal changes, and a history of confusion with various responses. When training is correct, external factors have less impact on the horse's behavior.

One of the tests of training is the new environment. Until now most of the work has taken place in the relatively homogeneous environment of the training arena. It may soon become clear that when the horse is ridden elsewhere, and is faced with changes in light and dark (such as shadows), water,

ditches, corners, walls—anywhere that it naturally wants to avoid—some degree of the basic responses may fly out of the window.

The horse needs to be trained in different places, and it generally requires about five separate environments for it to accustom to the new stimuli. Specific aspects, such as new water obstacles in horse trials, also require about five separate successful approaches. However, this suspicious tendency is genetically influenced, and some "bold" and "brave" horses may not show aversive responses in these situations. The average horse will already have balked at various obstacles, and so the training of "proof" requires the reinstallation and "shoring up" of the basic response qualities of timing, rhythm, and so on.

It is not only the go response that deteriorates in these new situations, but also the stop and turn responses. When the horse is finally trained to go into a shallow water crossing, it may be heavy to stop or turn. I once had to retrain a Thoroughbred horse during a clinic at Centennial Park Riding Centre in the heart of Sydney. For some years this horse had refused to cross one of two three-lane highways to reach the equestrian recreational park. When I finally trained the horse to step over the curb and on to the asphalt road, I had no control of the stop or turn responses until I reached the other side. I was skidding and skittering toward cars that were too close for comfort, and on the other side almost lost my right kneecap as the horse sideswiped a pole. In these foreign environments hyperreactive states are aroused and the hard-wired fleeing response is all that the horse can respond to. While there is a natural tendency for the horse to habituate to these environments over time, fleeing responses can overwhelm trained responses, and the latter need to be deliberately retrained in such "testing" environments.

Training the horse in these initially aversive environments deepens its basic responses. It helps ensure that the basic signal-response units are always functional and safe, whatever else is going on around the horse. Dog trainers use the term "proof" to imply that a trained dog should "sit on a hay bale in a hurricane" (as they say) if signaled to do so.

Riders and trainers frequently believe that diversifying training and "desensitizing" the horse to various environmental stimuli are more important than the thorough training of the basic responses. This is a misconception. The more thorough and the more consolidated the horse's basic training within the training arena, the easier it is to introduce it to new environments. A hyperreactive reaction in a new environment usually reflects the horse's conflict in the basic responses. It is essential to understand that what one sees as nervousness may in fact be confusion. "Horseshy" horses, for example, are generally just exhibiting confusion in their go/stop responses.

Certain aspects of "proof" are trained almost daily because of changes in weather and environmental features during training sessions. Training is, however, faster in homogeneous environments. Sooner or later it is necessary to diversify the training environment, and deepen the responses by training the horse to cross ditches, water, and so on calmly.

Left and below center *Maintaining speed in rhythm, straightness, and a light contact leads to a relaxed gallop. A "pulling" horse does not maintain its rhythm.*

Below *Racehorses maximize their potential if they are trained to gallop in self-carriage, and length of stride is enhanced when contact is light and the poll is highest.*

The gallop

The above blueprint applies to the training of walk, then trot, then canter. Racehorses and cross-country horses (eventers) also require training at the gallop particularly with respect to stop and go signals. The gallop requires a faster heartbeat than the slower paces; the increased level of adrenaline can "dampen" the quality of trained responses. It is poor training to maintain a permanently heavy contact with the horse's mouth; this will detrain the stop response and increase the horse's adrenaline levels. If the horse begins to rush at gallop, it pays to go back to slower gaits to work out where the loss of self-maintained speed or line or connection is occurring.

Then train the horse to maintain self-carriage at progressively faster speeds up to and including the gallop.

At the gallop the horse should be slowed with the reins the instant it rushes, and released the instant it shows any slowing. Strong pressure may be needed to slow the horse, and should be applied only for one stride (otherwise the horse is expressing slower strides that are unrewarded). Every random change in speed must be addressed. Lots of transitions into and out of the gallop should be performed.

There is no such thing as a "pulling" horse—it is the rider that pulls. If the horse is "pulling" it is because the clarity of the stop response has been lost and the rider maintains a heavy contact. Many transitions need to be done on the flat and while traveling at speed in order to reestablish the basic signals. Riders who pull against their horses' mouths should increase the pressure only until the horse has slowed, softening as soon as it gives a response. The pressure should be applied for only one stride.

There is potential for improvement of performance in horse racing using correct timing of the pressures in training, so that the horse is trained to accelerate unconditionally.

Roundness

I earlier described the development of roundness, when the horse is said to be "on the bit" (its neck is arched). This develops during training: A young and inexperienced horse does not immediately shorten its neck and tuck its head in as soon as the rider mounts. Roundness develops progressively through the complete and thorough acquisition of the responses of go, stop, turn the forelegs, and turn the hindlegs. It is trained only when the legs are fully controlled in timing; speed and rhythm; and line and straightness.

The first level of roundness—longitudinal flexion—occurs in the training of go and stop: the head and neck lower and soften. During the training of turn of the forelegs, lateral flexion develops; the horse now looks in and down (resulting in more roundness than before), but still looks loose and relatively long in the frame. Finally, the development of the turn of the hindquarters as it goes through the qualities adds further to roundness and raises the poll, developing collection.

Consolidation of responses

The horse requires repetition and practice to develop clear habits. Most of all it requires time. Too many responses too quickly can mentally tire a young or inexperienced horse. It doesn't matter whether training takes place every day: The most important aspects are clarity and absence of conflict.

Consolidation of foundation training in the young horse takes a few months. Turning the horse out to pasture for a spell after four to nine weeks of training (depending on its progress, behavior, and physiology) hastens consolidation. Some young horses need turning out after only a few weeks in work, as they are too mentally or physically immature to continue, and progress falters. If the reinforcement process has been carried out properly, however, horses forget none of their training, even after years. By the same token, if they are turned out with associated hyperreactive responses, these too tend to be retained.

Correctly trained horses usually return from a break in training as good as or better than when they left in terms of their trained responses, because of the consolidation that occurs during the rest period. Some trainers believe that during the turn-out the horse "thinks" about its training, but this is unlikely given what we know about the horse's mental processes. Rather, the consolidation is the result of the maturation of newly laid-down neural pathways in the horse's brain.

PROGRESSIVE TRAINING: JUMPING

Jumping is excellent training for all horses, regardless of the discipline for which they are ultimately intended. Training "non-jumping" horses (such as dressage horses) to jump is sometimes referred to as cross-training. Jumping is a very good test of the depth of the qualities of the basic responses under saddle, and will very quickly show up any flaws in training. Any problems encountered while jumping should be addressed as failures of forward or stop, and not as idiosyncrasies of the individual horse ("unwillingness") or any other aspects of its "personality." A closer scrutiny of jumping problems shows that these too are associated with quickening, slowing, or offering no response.

All horses can be trained to jump reliably over many different types of obstacles, and riders should focus on the training of the jumping response rather than relying on the natural ability or so-called "desire" of the horse to jump. Older horses that may already have learned evasions can be trained to jump reliably using the same techniques as for young horses. Unfortunately, many of the cures used for problems encountered when jumping unwittingly reward the very behaviors they wish to eradicate.

The ultimate goal in early training is for the horse to be able to negotiate a small course of obstacles with reliable speed and rhythm, maintaining a central track to each obstacle, and self-carriage in the natural outline.

Jumping equipment does not need to be fancy to be effective but it does need to be safe; obstacles should be sturdy but collapse when knocked. They should have no sharp edges. The arena surface should be even, not too deep, and definitely not slippery. The rider needs to be balanced enough to allow the horse a range of unexpected movements without accidentally jerking on the reins and inadvertently giving incorrect cues. Throughout jump training the rider must allow the horse plenty of freedom of neck and head so that it can stretch forward over the obstacle and maintain self-carriage at all times.

The basis of jumping training lies in the horse's ability to negotiate obstacles without losing the qualities of its responses (go, stop, turn). It is probably of great advantage to the horse that it is not capable of analyzing its responses in the way that humans do. The downside of this is that the horse that is trained to jump only one water jump will not, when it sees another one, be able to reason: "Aha, another water jump!" It needs to have successfully negotiated about five separate examples of water jump before the rider can assume that it will recognize that particular type of obstacle. This type of thinking should be applied to all aspects of jumping training, including the patterns and colors on show-jumping poles, different types of obstacles, and different types of arena.

Training over poles on the ground

Jump training commences with walking the horse over single poles on the ground, placed randomly around the arena.

It is important that the horse begins at the walk, in the natural outline, and is trained through all the qualities of go, stop, and the turn of the forelegs over the poles. This includes "adjustability": The horse must learn to shorten and lengthen the stride between closely and widely spaced poles to be sure that the rider's signals control the horse's behavior. Any deterioration in the basic signals should be addressed immediately. When all is complete at the walk, the trot is tested and trained for all qualities. There is no need for canter at this stage; it is less controllable over a given distance, as the strides are much longer and can allow hyperreactivity to creep in unnoticed. In retraining, however, the canter may be necessary over poles if the horse has

learned hyperreactive associations or balking at this gait. Transitions are used to train the horse to maintain its timing, rhythm, and line over the poles. It is then trained to maintain its connection and outline over a series of poles scattered throughout the training area. Finally, longer and shorter strides are trained. When this is achieved successfully, the horse is ready to begin jumping small obstacles.

Dealing with balking

If the horse balks at the poles, it should never be punished. Its head should be maintained facing the pole; any turning away steps should be corrected with an opposite turn step signal/pressure. The horse must never be turned in the direction in which it veered.

The pressures for go must not be relaxed until the horse steps forward. The outcome is that the horse goes over the pole, but remember that it is

1 When the horse can demonstrate self-maintained speed over the pole, line and straightness are trained.

2 The horse should also be able to trot over poles in the natural outline without speed alterations. Here it has slowed a little.

3 When the horse drifts and quickens, rein pressure is used to correct it. When the horse drifts and slows, stronger leg pressure on the bulging side is used. In jumping, as with other saddle work, rein and leg pressure should not be used simultaneously.

the horse experiences, the more likely it is to occur in the future. Gradually increasing the size of the obstacles, with many successful repetitions, is the most effective way to train the horse to jump larger obstacles. The horse needs to incorporate each new obstacle height into its stock of learned responses.

Correct basic jumping training will have far-reaching implications for the horse's future jumping career, and no aspect should be rushed or missed. It is accepted by most riders that some horses are more motivated to avoid knocking rails than others, and while there is definitely a genetic influence here there is a strong training component too. A horse that does not offer clear, light responses to the rider's signals, or one that exhibits the flight response in any significant way, is far more likely to knock rails than one that is correctly trained. Confused, tense horses are less sensitive to external stimuli. The relaxed horse that is clearly trained in pressure/response is far more likely to find the knocking of the poles with its forelegs aversive (and thus alter its behavior) than the horse that has habituated to heavy aids or exhibits flight response.

Jumping spreads

All spreads involve two key components: multiple rails at the highest point of the obstacle, and an empty void between the rails. The horse should be trained to associate the jumping response both with the rails and with the space between. These are best trained separately.

To train multiple poles, two vertical jumping obstacles involving four wings are positioned very

Left If the horse balks at the poles, it should not be turned away. The training of the go response should follow the principles and timing of negative reinforcement.

simply the go response that is being trained—the pole is incidental—so every correct step must be reinforced with release. Sometimes, in retraining, the tapping of the dressage whip is required to elicit go: Here the principles of negative reinforcement should be maintained and applied. It is important not to let the horse turn away from the pole because if this removes the pole from the horse's visual field and puts distance between the horse and the pole, the horse remembers the turn away as successfully solving the problem.

Training over jumps

The next stage is to tackle low rails, no more than a few inches above the ground. As soon as the height of the fence requires a jumping effort, however, walk is abandoned and trot is the slowest gait to be trained, otherwise rhythm is sacrificed. Cross-rails can also be introduced. Once again, the priority is to maintain the clarity of the basic training and to progress in the natural outline in self-carriage through all the qualities.

Obstacle heights or spreads should be raised slowly, with plenty of practice at each new height. By adding only a few inches at a time, the difference between the new height and the previous one is barely noticeable. The horse may initially make contact with the rail at the new height, but by trial and error will learn to jump cleanly. The same applies to spreads. "Overfacing," or attempting to jump obstacles that are too large for the horse's level of training, is very detrimental as it often leads to refusals or run-outs (the new heights do not compute with what is stored in memory about the obstacle). It is commonly believed that overfacing destroys a horse's confidence, but actually it increases the likelihood that the horse will successfully trial either running out or refusing. The more of this behavior

Below When the horse is able to walk and trot over ground-rails with basic qualities intact it is ready to trot up to cross-rails.

Right top *The basic shapes that train the horse's initial jumping responses of width and height are cross-rails, oxers, and the simple vertical.*

Right center *To further train or retrain jumping responses that involve multiple top rails, very narrow oxers can be constructed and raised accordingly.*

Right below *When a low front rail is separated from a higher back rail by a significant gap, the width component of spread fences is isolated for training. Dimensions can be increased.*

Above *When width training is complete the oxer can be built so that width is similar to height.*

close together, say 8 inches (20 cm) apart, to make a parallel "oxer." This single obstacle is set lower than the height the horse is jumping comfortably. As the horse is successful over this, maintaining all qualities of the go response, the obstacle is gradually widened until the width is slightly greater than the height. Jumping such wider obstacles is generally more easily achieved at the canter; care must be taken to ensure that all response qualities remain intact.

To train the picture of the wider empty-looking obstacle, two vertical obstacles are brought together, one almost at ground level, the other significantly higher. The low one is on the approach side, and the distance between the two is at least the height of the higher rail.

Most spread obstacles that the horse encounters consist of some amalgamation of these two obstacles,

1 *The rider is slightly behind the movement and is falling backward.*

2 *The rider's hands should allow the neck to stretch, and if the rider is experienced, maintain contact. The rider should fold at the hips and the lower leg should remain unchanged.*

and once stimulus generalization has occurred new spread obstacles will not be aversive.

Rider position

There are many books and many trainers that effectively teach rider position over fences. Position is very important, as a rider with a set of reins in his hands can easily and inadvertently punish the jumping response. The basics of good rider position involve:

- folding at the hip joint (leaning forward) during the acceleration of the jumping effort (on takeoff)
- unfolding as the horse descends
- releasing some rein so that the horse is able to stretch its neck. Highly skilled riders are capable of maintaining the contact while allowing the horse's neck to stretch
- maintaining the normal position of the lower leg (the calf) on the horse's sides during the jumping effort

Turning away and refusing

When the horse turns or spins away from the obstacle, it must immediately be prevented from continuing or forming a circle. The rider must instantly apply the opposite turning rein and bring the shoulders back onto line, then apply the go signal and pressure until the horse goes forward. Even if the horse steps through

the collapsible obstacle, next time it will pick up its feet and jump.

If the horse's training is correct with respect to all its basic responses, and jumping training is progressive, it will not learn to turn away or refuse. Therefore maintaining the horse at the obstacle when it has refused is in the realm of retraining, and only experienced jumping riders should attempt to do this. The horse should, ideally, never learn to turn away (run out) from a obstacle, but should be made to step over it from walk or halt. Refusals are the result of slowing or quickening problems in a horse's jumping response. Retraining rhythm is the solution to this problem.

3 *The rider is in front of the movement, affecting the rhythm of takeoff. The rider is gripping with the knees, destabilizing the lower leg.*

The common practice of punishing the horse at the base of the fence when it has refused, then turning it away, is only marginally effective. Because the application of the whip is not immediately followed by a forward step or jump, but by a turn away, it simply reinforces turning away. The application of the whip may result in a jump effort in the short term, but the jump will be an expression of flight response rather than a trained forward response. Horses can be trained to be what jumping riders term "honest" as easily as they can be taught to be habitual refusers. Even an Olympic show jumper could be trained *not* to jump if it was made to approach an obstacle, then swerved away from it enough times.

The notion of the "eager" horse is also a product of our anthropomorphic belief system. Horses that habitually rush obstacles are often described as being overly eager to jump, when they are actually exhibiting the flight response in relation to jumping. Horses that rush obstacles usually rush away from them with just the same level of "enthusiasm."

It is important to view jumping disobediences as failures of go and stop, and address these deficiencies before attempting any retraining. The most useful technique when retraining horses to jump is "under-riding." Generally this refers to a mistake on the rider's part where the horse is presented at an obstacle too slowly and without power. However, here I use it as a positive tool to retrain a horse that fails to jump. This can be useful for horses that refuse or run out, as it singles out the horse's learned jumping response from a signal and excludes any element of the flight response, fence association, speed, gait, or momentum. It should only be attempted by skilled jumping riders.

1 The horse has refused an obstacle that is sufficiently low for it to retake without turning away and re-negotiating the line.

To begin, a vertical obstacle that offers the lowest but nevertheless significant temptation to the horse to refuse is chosen. This can be up to about 30 inches (80 cm) high if the rider is capable. For safety's sake, the cups that hold the rail should be flat so that the rail falls easily. The horse is ridden at a too slow trot toward the fence, and when it stops, is pressured to go. The pressure may need to be increased with whip taps and maintained for some seconds until finally the horse "trials" the jump effort. The rider must be skilled enough to fold instantly and not hinder the horse's balance or mouth. The horse can even be walked toward the obstacle, or halted 6 feet (2 m) away from it. Then the go signal is applied, and again at the point of takeoff. If the horse attempts to run out, correct it quickly and do not allow it to turn its head away from the obstacle and lose focus. The rider increases the pressure of the go signal until the horse jumps over the obstacle. After one awkward jump the horse rapidly improves as he learns that stopping is no longer reinforced. Soon the horse will respond to the "timing" of the squeezing leg signal that encourages the takeoff.

Right *Under-riding is a technique used to remedy habitual refusing. By carefully using principles and timing of negative reinforcement, the horse is pressured to make the jumping efforts from halt at close quarters. This also results in the horse becoming comfortable close to the obstacle.*

2 As the horse attempts to turn away to the right, the rider brings it back on line with the left rein.

> *Horses that habitually rush obstacles are often described as loving to jump or as being overly eager to jump, when they are actually exhibiting the flight response in relation to jumping.*

3 Preventing any further random attempt to turn right, the rider is ready to pressure the left rein, and then pressure forward until the horse completes the obstacle.

When the horse is jumping reliably, which takes only a few repetitions, it is time to address the running away after the jump. A slowing transition to walk or even halt is applied after landing, with an obvious instant release afterward. Line is then addressed, and angles trained and tested; the horse becomes progressively calmer. After a couple of correct repetitions the stimulus/response relationship has been reconnected and the horse is very relaxed: It is now working within clear boundaries. People are constantly amazed at how this technique has the power to transform a previously tense horse that refused obstacles.

Under-riding should only be practiced with vertical obstacles, or very narrow spread obstacles (up to 8 inches [20 cm] wide), because of the extra power required to take off with low or zero momentum.

Wider spreads should be retrained at the canter, beginning with obstacles with lower front rails. Only very experienced jumping riders should attempt this training.

Shaping the jumping response

1 Basic attempt

At this stage of the horse's training over raised obstacles, the Basic attempt refers to a possibly crude but nonetheless successful negotiation of the obstacle. The horse learns not to turn away or refuse outright, but to make an attempt, regardless of its quality. We have

> *...in the retraining situation, hyperreactive responses...may be incorporated into the horse's jumping habits.*

already reviewed the reasons why the horse should not be allowed to turn away from an obstacle. There are, however, a few exceptions to this rule, as follows:

- when the obstacle is too high for horse or rider to negotiate it safely and smoothly
- when the obstacle is too wide for horse or rider to negotiate it safely and smoothly (most spreads are)
- when the obstacle is solid and the top rail cannot be dislodged
- when the horse is too close to a tall obstacle
- when the footing is unsuitable
- when the horse is excessively hyperreactive (although this may be due in part to the refusal)

If the horse rushes backward out of obstacles it becomes far more fearful of them and much harder to retrain, so it is crucial that the rider increases the pressure when the horse is almost over or through the obstacle to ensure that it goes forward.

2 Timing

Now that the horse is jumping reliably, it may be noticed that the jumping effort is barely enough to clear the obstacle—it is not powerful. There may even be a stalling at the base of the obstacle. Now it is time to ensure that the closing of the rider's legs has an immediate response on the horse's hindlegs. It is also time to train a clearer steady response from the reins

on landing—not to stop, but just to steady the horse. During jumping the rider's leg should never be permanently clamped on. It is used only for a go transition (which includes the jumping effort since the jump is a transition requiring more power than the preceding strides). If the leg applied at the base of the obstacle is insufficient to empower the jump effort, then a single *very light* whip tap can be applied on the horse's rib cage on takeoff.

3 Speed and rhythm

If the timing qualities of the go and stop responses are correct, the horse should maintain a constant speed and rhythm. However, in the retraining situation, hyperreactive responses and learned slowing, stalling responses may be incorporated into the horse's jumping habits. Hyperreactive responses should be trained error-free—they should be deleted with appropriate transitions, because their expression can lead to problems such as rushing, which causes a further deterioration in jumping and leads to knocking rails, the pain of which leads to more hyperreactivity, and so on—a vicious circle.

If the horse changes pace over the early training obstacles, transitions to the next gait above or below following each obstacle eventually result in a consistent speed and rhythm. The rider should be careful when using the reins to avoid any interference with the horse at the takeoff point as the horse will alter its rhythm and may even learn to refuse.

In the case of a severe rushing problem, the timing disappears and the horse is no longer light to slow. The rider needs just to steady it on the approach to the obstacle, but on the landing side do a strong

transition to halt within 16 feet (5 m). Most horses that rush learn to do it initially by running away from the obstacle. The cause may be the pain of hitting a rail, or the discomfort caused by poor riding, especially with respect to the mouth connection. Doing halt transitions from trot at the 16 feet (5 m) mark is made even more effective as a training tool if the horse is first trained to skid-stop (one beat of the rhythm rather than three). The horse soon loses its tendency to rush away from the obstacle and becomes more controllable in its speed of approach.

When jumping from trot, prevent the horse from departing the obstacle faster than it approached. This quickening may be a hyperreactive response, or may result in one.

4 Line and straightness

Any drift should be corrected using the techniques described earlier in this chapter, training the shoulders first. The precise correction required depends on the associated slowing or quickening. At this stage the horse can also be trained to approach obstacles at an angle, gradually increasing the degree. Line and straightness should also be tested and trained over related lines of, and narrower, obstacles.

5 Connection and outline

The maintenance of a constant connection and outline over a series of obstacles is tested and any deviations corrected. Here again, any problems may have associated speed changes.

6 Adjustability

At this stage the horse is ready to be shortened and lengthened in the stride from the leg and rein signals respectively, as described over the poles on the ground (see p. 126). The seat of the rider becomes increasingly associated with the rein responses by this stage, thus the bracing seat (sitting deeper and more upright) will have some effect in slowing the horse. Any deterioration in previous qualities is retrained.

7 Proof

Once the horse is negotiating cross-rails calmly it can be introduced to small (1-foot/30-cm) obstacles of the types it is likely to encounter in competition: planks, walls, drums, brush, oxers, and so on. It is important to diversify the horse's experience as far as possible through the gradual introduction of new obstacles and training environments.

Cantering over obstacles

Once the horse is calmly negotiating small obstacles of various types at trot, the canter can be introduced. Obstacles should be spaced so that the horse can easily manage at least three straight (nonturning) strides before and after each jumping effort. If the

Left *Cross-country training involves training the horse to jump a variety of obstacles.*

Above Losses of line and straightness are associated with losses of speed. This can cause stalling and further problems in jumping.

However, there are important differences in the nature and variety of obstacles on the cross-country course, in particular ditches, small banks, drops, and water obstacles, as well as tests of accuracy such as arrowheads and corners (apexes). These are all most efficiently trained in smaller dimensions. Banks, ditches, and water should be negotiated at walk, preventing the horse from turning away and using clear pressure/release training to ensure that it goes forward.

Horses have an instinctive fear of ditches, water, and so on, because historically they would have been more likely to encounter predators there. Punishing the horse for not going into the water will not make the problem go away. Instead use clear negative reinforcement principles to elicit each forward step.

The rider should also pay particular attention to speed and rhythm. As with show jumping, begin with low obstacles and train at the trot. Any rushing steps should be thwarted with rein signals and pressures and downward transitions. Riders who pay little attention to a tendency to rush over ditches, up and down banks, and through water are misinterpreting what the rushing represents—hyperreactive fear responses. While such a horse may take its career to high levels, there is a significant chance that it will unexpectedly refuse an obstacle as the degree of difficulty increases, or when a closer takeoff is required. Rushing horses vary the positions of their takeoff points considerably, and so are

qualities of the basic responses show any deterioration they should be progressively retrained.

Generally speaking, the rider should attempt to ride the horse more forward on the turns to prevent its natural tendency to slow and lose power from the inside hind leg around the corners. As soon as the turn is complete and the straight track toward the obstacle appears, the rider should steady the horse and maintain its poll higher than the rest of the neck in order to keep its center of gravity further back toward the hindquarters. At the base of the obstacle the rider softens the rein connection and applies the leg signals.

Cross-country jumping

Jumping most cross-country obstacles is no more than an elaboration of the "proof" component of show- or stadium-jumping training. The horse is trained to jump cross-country in exactly the same way as is is trained to jump, except that, with greater speed, the horse learns how to take off and land at considerably longer distances from the obstacle.

Left *Young horses can be trained over obstacles at walk to consolidate speed and rhythm qualities. The stop and go responses should be able to be effective at any moment, within reason.*

unfamiliar with the closer takeoffs necessary for certain types of obstacle such as rising spreads and tiger traps.

Rushing in show jumping is dangerous for both horse and rider, but in cross-country it can be fatal. A significant proportion of deaths in the sport are associated with horses that rush at jumps. This is the most disastrous aspect of the anthropomorphic approach to horse behavior—the benevolent horse that "wants to please" its owner, the "eager" horse that rushes its jumps because it loves jumping so much (yet it never seems to practice this over a course in its paddock).

Horses that rush are hyperreactive. Hyperreactive horses are not happy; they are fearful in every sense of the word. Yet in all the reams written in search of an explanation for the all-too-high death rate of riders in eventing (to say nothing of horse deaths), little mention is made of training. Training horses to have a self-maintained rhythm or cruise control, where the rider can release the reins for a stride or two without any change in speed, would prevent much of the carnage.

> *For when the correct order of riding is not understood and the moderating effect of the hand is unknown, or else by too much impatience temporarily suspended, horses are brought to such a state that they care neither for hand nor spur, for bit nor cavesson...and a feeling creature is made into a senseless block.*

The Art of Riding, John Astley (1584)

CHAPTER 8 AVOIDING CONFLICT

THE HISTORY OF HORSEMANSHIP IS STREWN WITH TALES OF HORSES THAT RESISTED TRAINING SO VIGOROUSLY THAT THEY WERE DEEMED UNRIDEABLE, MAD, OR JUST PLAIN MEAN. EVERYONE HAS THEIR OWN STORY ABOUT A DIFFICULT, TENSE, OR AGGRESSIVE HORSE.

A vast arsenal of pharmaceutical, herbal, and dietary solutions awaits the unlucky owner of such a beast, not to mention innumerable training manuals, videos, and gadgets, including electrical collars that claim to cure various vices.

Among the many reasons proposed for problem behavior are genetic predisposition; instinctively driven behavior (such as separation anxiety); hormones; environmental events; dietary deficiencies and overloads; traumatic events in past history; poor conformation; and more. All these factors can certainly *contribute* to incorrect behavior, but they are almost never the *sole cause*. Genetics, for example, might *predispose* an animal to behave in a certain way, but such behaviors are only *confirmed* or *denied* by learning and repetition. Other reasons frequently cited for problem behavior include mood swings, bad attitudes, naughtiness, revenge, and stupidity. These are all incorrect interpretations of what are essentially conflict behaviors. This realization not only throws a whole new light on problem behaviors; it also makes the prospect of fixing them far more achievable. Most importantly, it has the potential to lower failure rates, and the associated wastage of horses.

In my early dealings with equine conflict behaviors, I too embraced the justifications of genes, attitude, and so on; at that time science had made few inroads into training and there were simply no other interpretations available. But my experiences with a huge range of "problem" horses over the decades have completely altered the way in which I view horse behavior and training.

I noticed that the more skilled I became in foundation training, the more similar the horses would end up, no matter how much they had differed at the start of the course. Any problems they ended up with were as a result of my training. Horses arriving at our center for retraining, however, displayed a huge range of differences from the word go. Why should one group of horses show remarkable similarities in behavior on finishing foundation training, yet another group exhibit huge variations in behavior on arrival for retraining? The only reasonable explanation appeared to be that the behavior we regarded as problematic had in fact been learned.

Most horse owners I see for retraining describe their animal in terms that imply it "knows" what it is doing wrong. This approach to problem behavior can give rise to a similar mind-set in retraining: If the horse does not improve, it's the horse's fault; the trainer is exempt from blame. This anthropomorphic mind-set can frequently lead to retributive styles of training, or training that is unrelated to the original stimulus-response failure—it requires the horse to understand its misbehavior and take the appropriate steps to correct itself. During assessments and retraining, however, predictable patterns emerge that show a clear relationship between the behavior and the learned responses.

What is conflict behavior?

Conflict behavior occurs when the horse is "torn" between responses. In human terms you might say that it cannot make up its mind about how to respond to a given signal. For the horse it's not a free-will choice, but much more like cross-wiring on an electrical circuit. The problem is exacerbated by the horse's lack of analytical ability to sort things out for itself.

Below *Bucking is a conflict relating to the "go" signal, and eventually the "stop" also deteriorates as a result. The rider leans forward for the leap then back for the buck. He attempts to apply stop, followed immediately by go signals.*

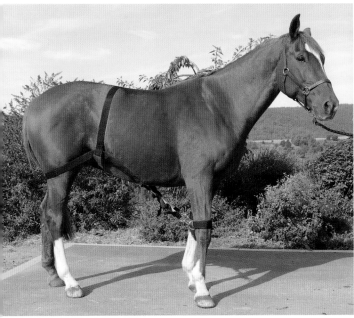

When trainers give confusing messages, the horse's brain directs its body to get away from the situation. In nature this is easy; in training it is generally impossible. In the horse's brain, adrenaline, cortisol, and other chemicals are released to prepare the body for flight, and the animal reaches a state of extreme tension, or hyperreactivity. The more hyperreactivity it expresses, particularly if it can move its legs quickly, the more the tension overwhelms its body and brain. It also has the effect of "switching off" trained responses; it is more important to escape than to be overwhelmed by—and possibly succumb to—an attack by a predator. This switching off is why bolting horses don't stop or turn too easily. It's not that they won't; it's more that they just don't register.

Horses recover fully from periodic episodes of tension. But when an animal is exposed over a long period to a stressful situation that it cannot flee, chronic stress arises. This presents as raised cortico-steroid levels, frequent manifestation of the flight response, physiological disturbances, stomach damage (including ulcers and colic in horses), repetition and ritualization of original conflict behaviors, increased and redirected aggression, development of stereotypies (windsucking, wood chewing, tongue lolling, paddock and stall walking, and weaving), and injurious behaviors such as self-mutilation.

Conflict behavior is probably a population adaptiveness control measure. Those animals that cannot interact with their environment become less "fit" and have lower reproductive success. In nature animals generally dovetail with this world. In training it is up to us to ensure this happens.

How conflict shows up

The horse has a genetic tendency to trial various responses to stimuli. If it is unable to free itself from pressure, or produce consistent responses to stimuli in training, the flight response is initiated and conflict behaviors occur. Many horses trial hyperreactive postures (such as high head carriage) or behaviors (tension, running, quickening); many trial the flight response when confusion strikes. The more the horse practices it, the more severe it can become. Thus rearing, bucking, bolting, shying, excessive tension, "girthiness," extreme headshyness, aggression,

Far left This device restrains the legs of a horse that kicks the trailer and won't stand still. In fact the horse is simply confused about signals and responses.
Above *Some questionable contraptions have been invented to force a rounded outline and simultaneously activate the hindlegs.*
Left *Other devices are claimed to cure behaviors, but in fact punish symptoms rather than retrain the causes of problems.*

learning process. In a famous experiment, he used food rewards to train dogs to discriminate between a circle and an ellipse whereby one shape was punished and the other rewarded. He then gradually merged the two shapes until the dogs could no longer tell the two apart. This induced various expressions of neurosis in the dogs: Some became extremely aggressive and agitated; others responded randomly to all stimuli irrespective of shape, while still others stopped responding altogether and fell asleep. Most were unable to participate in the experiment any further.

Uniformity of responses in nature

In nature, animals perceive an association between environmental stimuli and their own responses, as well as between their own behavior and subsequent events. For example, an animal learns that the call of a certain bird precedes the arrival of a predator that elicits running away; or a foal learns that demonstrating aggressive behavior toward other foals results in him acquiring more food. These signal-response relationships evolved to enable animals to survive in their natural environment.

When a given signal always leads to the same response, the neural pathway defining the association is reinforced and the response becomes predictable; this in turn gives the animal a level of controllability of its behavioral world. When with repeated practice the association becomes highly reliable, a stable behavior pattern emerges where actions transform into habits. As things become more predictable the animal's anxiety lowers and in this its behavior patterns become stable.

Above *Training clear stop and go signals via correct timing principles of negative reinforcement is the remedy for the leaping, bucking, bolting horse.*
Right *Manifest signs of tension are a raised head (this also indicates that the horse does not stop from a light signal), wide eyes, and flared nostrils. When the horse learns to stop from a light rein signal, its head will lower.*

overreactivity, and severe head-tossing, all of which incorporate aspects of the flight response, are all part of the hyperreactive rollercoaster. Mild expressions of the flight response will show up as stiffness through the body, short choppy steps, teeth grinding, and mild head tossing, but these can rapidly escalate to more severe behaviors.

A prime contributor to incorrect behaviors in training is the tendency of trainers to unwittingly reward the wrong ones, creating a vicious cycle. Hyperreactive states are not only commonly rewarded, but also loudly recommended in teachings and texts. "Ride the horse through his tension—he'll soon give it up" and "He's just playing—let him get it out of his system on the lunge," are just two of the entrenched—but wrongheaded—maxims that abound.

Conflict behavior in other species

Conflicts arising from inconsistent stimulus-response relationships have long been appreciated and understood to have dramatic effects on behavior. Pavlov was the first to explain the effects of confusion in the

> *A prime contributor to incorrect behaviors in training is the tendency of trainers to unwittingly reward the wrong ones, creating a vicious cycle.*

Possibly the most complex responses that horses learn are social ones. Horses live in social groups. Competition for resources between individuals varies throughout the year and throughout the animal's life. Relationships between individuals change. This means fitting in with the changing hierarchy, and choices, based on reward and punishment, have to be made.

Horses have evolved abilities to solve the challenges presented by their environment. What they have not evolved is the ability to produce uniform responses in training. The responsibility of making that happen lies with the trainer.

Uniformity of responses in training

The production of uniform responses in the horse has been the aim of all training systems through the centuries. During training, horses will offer a range of reponses, of varying qualities; these have to be progressively "shaped" until they become uniform. Small amounts of conflict behavior may emerge in the process. The qualities of responses are trained in a set order, beginning with the most random and ending with the ones of lowest "wildness."

Achieving consistency of response is not simple; the horse may trial all kinds of behavior, including:

- the "wrong" response
- delays in response
- variations in reactivity, including hyperreactivity
- alterations of speed
- alterations in direction
- alterations in body posture, such as head carriage

Uniform responses to discrete signals make the animal's world predictable and controllable. In

Left *In nature, the horse's world is predictable and controllable. We must make signals clear and consistent so that we do not undermine this predictability and cause stress and subsequent conflict.*
Below *In the horse's world, there are no crazy horses, and when short-term conflicts are resolved, calmness reigns.*

Above In new stressful situations, horses tend to become hyperreactive and try to flee. Training light stop and go signals and immobility resolves such tension.

Below When horses are consolidated in their basic training, even stallions can be signaled and controlled by children.

nature, signals that are only weakly attached to the animal's behavioral responses tend to be extinguished. In training, conflict behaviors arise when these weaker signals are not extinguished, because the rider keeps on eliciting them. The extent of the conflict is directly proportional to the reliability of the signal-response relationship. The stronger the attachment of signals to responses, the calmer the animal.

Training uniform responses makes the horse calmer simply because it is now not going to practice any hyperreactive responses. The less fear that the animal experiences, the quieter it becomes. The more fear it expresses, the more "trigger-happy" the flight response.

Causes of conflict

1 Opposing signals

Stop and go are opposing responses, so applying rein and leg signals together (in horses that are unable to habituate to the mouth discomfort) can result in conflict behavior. Even those that habituate end up with heavy responses and rein contact; riders assume this to be normal. However, for the horse the heavy contact may be ample reason for conflict behavior.

Conflicts that arise from opposing pressures are generally more severe in expression than other causes, and therefore more damaging. Go and stop conflicts frequently present as rearing, bucking, shying, bolting, separation anxiety, fence walking, and even self-mutilation. These conflicts are also seen in lungeing where side reins constrain the horse's head so that the face plane is vertical or behind the vertical.

2 General confusion

Training random, nonuniform responses; issuing too many signals for a single response; training a single signal to elicit multiple responses; signaling two or more responses at once before consolidation; no release of pressure or release at the wrong time—all these actions contribute to conflict, and generally result in hyperreactivity, or (depending on the horse's predisposition), dullness and "laziness." Horses frequently "switch off" if the sum total of conflicts is high. Trainers should concentrate on the qualities of timing, speed and rhythm, line and straightness, and connection and outline to improve uniformity of responses and thereby avoid confusion.

3 Natural equine tendencies

Horses may sometimes become aggressive toward their human handlers. This is not a lack of respect but a sign of conflict in trained responses. Obedient horses, including stallions, do not show aggression toward humans. There may be instances—perhaps during a rising level of nutrition, in a particular season or breeding cycle, or after an interaction with another horse (redirected aggression)—when a horse may trial aggressive behavior toward humans. This will usually show up as a ritualized threat posture, such as laying the ears back. If the human retreats during such a threat, the behavior is reinforced and thus repeated. It is important that any such tendency be retrained in hand.

My view is that stallions are aggressive because they are trained to be that way, generally inadvertently, by having their early expressions of aggression reinforced. I have owned, trained, and competed on many types of stallions, and all were extremely placid after initial handling and riding. The benevolent model of horse behavior, and our tendency to "humanize" horses, result in stallions receiving training that is designed to "show them who is boss." The consequences of this are clear enough: Every "vicious" stallion I have ever met has been riddled with conflict behaviors, as shown by poor responses in hand and under saddle. And an

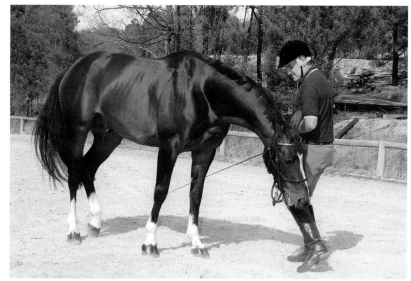

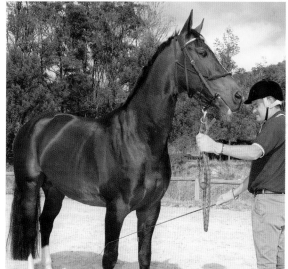

Above, left and below
The death rate in stallions during training is high because of their evolved tendencies to undermine social responses and attempt to assert their own control. Clear training is vital to ensuring that they respond appropriately to a range of light signal pressures.

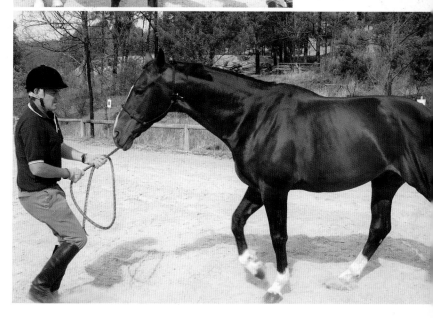

1 *As the horse is ridden toward a frightening obstacle (a bridge) it begins to stall and swerve. The rider requests a step at a time, and deviations of line are corrected with the reins.*

2 *The horse may sniff the object, but if it steps back, the rider must make the horse step forward again.*

appallingly high percentage of performance stallions die of colic rather than old age (see p. 39).

4 Avoidance behavior

Horses vary in their aversions; some will go without hesitation toward completely unfamiliar objects, while others may balk. This is evident in early interactions with young horses, and early training has the power to confirm or delete these tendencies. In addition, poorly trained "go" responses may present as stalling, swerving, shying, and rearing, regardless of genetic predisposition.

When horses are allowed to veer away from objects, the resulting loss of uniformity of response to signals can cause conflict behavior to develop. These random behaviors generally present as hyperreactive responses. For example, the trail horse that sidesteps puddles, water, shadows, and small logs may soon (but not always) develop faster versions of these responses that result in shying.

Shying usually develops from "go" problems. The horse slows and loses its focus straight ahead; after a few repetitions it stalls; soon it begins to turn away; then it turns away faster; finally it may learn to run away a few or many steps. The response has four components: During the split-second reaction of shying, the horse first stalls, then looks away, then turns the shoulders away, then finally runs away. Shying behavior is most rapidly learned when it involves complete escape. This reinforcement is compounded by the incremental loss of control by the rider, as the horse develops worsening shying behavior.

Right *Responses such as balking then running away can escalate to bigger and quicker efforts of leaping and bounding away if the rider is unable to stop the horse effectively with the reins.*

With practice, shying can also result in rearing (which can originate from mild turn-away behavior or full-blown shying). The origin seems to depend on genetic predisposition and training history. During the intermediate stages of development, the behavior is frequently a mixture of shy and rear. Therefore almost all rearing horses tend to change their original

144

3 Successful turn-away responses may develop into faster spinning away. The rider attempts to maintain turn rein-pressure.

4 Spinning may develop into a yet faster response—rearing away. The rider resumes the turn-right signal when the horse is stable on both hindlegs.

5 When these go and turn issues are resolved, the horse stands on the bridge relaxed.

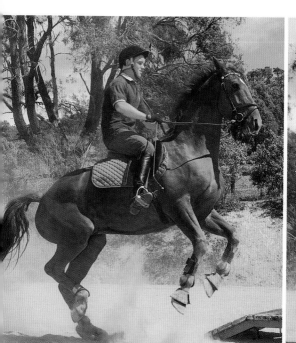

> *Shying behavior is most rapidly learned when it involves complete escape. This reinforcement is compounded by the incremental loss of control by the rider.*

direction: Most tend to land left. Correction of rearing involves correction of line (right rein) and then go (both legs).

At first jibbing (stalling), shying, and rearing tend to occur with certain context-specific associations. Soon, however, they are practiced anywhere and without any obvious stimulus, and the horse begins to lose some qualities of go and stop. Jibbing and shying can develop into unpredictably practiced behaviors when reinforced by facing away, turning away, and running away.

During jumping training, horses learn to avoid obstacles through stalling (usually between the last and take-off stride). This may be preempted by habitual losses of rhythm and tempo or directional line. Outright refusal is generally the next step, which is why proficient jumping trainers insist on riders maintaining rhythm and line. When horses refuse obstacles outright, turning them away reinforces the refusal; the horse learns that the turn-away made the obstacle disappear. It generally attempts to repeat the turn in the same direction when next presented at the obstacle.

5 Accidental experiences

Shying and running away can also result from something accidental. For example, a dog may suddenly emerge unannounced from the undergrowth. The horse expresses aversive behavior and at the same time perceives that the rider loses balance, grip, connection, and control. A horse may therefore rapidly learn to repeat these behaviors, especially if it experiences a number of similar events. This behavior is generally place-dependent at first, but may escalate to new sites with repetition and reinforcement.

6 Pain

Pain may arise from physical injuries, physiological disturbances, ill-fitting gear, or maintained pressure from the rider's hands or legs. It may result from punishment, especially violent retributive measures. This may lead to the development of various levels of conflict behavior, varying from bridle lameness (irregular rhythm causing rein-connection conflicts) to self-mutilation in particularly severe cases. Generally, it becomes clear during the process of behavior modification whether pain is the underlying cause. The trial use of analgesics can give a useful indication: If the problem persists despite the use of analgesics, then the underlying issue is likely to be behavioral, rather than pain-related.

7 Poor conformation

The structural conformation of horses predisposes them to certain tasks. Wither-high horses tend to be more capable in dressage and jumping; croup-high horses tend to be faster sprinters. Unsound conformation (cow hocks, sickle hocks, straight hindlegs, base narrow, base wide, bench knees, calf knees, back at the knee, swaybacks, roach backs, backs that are too long or too short) also affects the abilities of performance horses. Training horses with some conformational defects can result in conflict because the animal is simply not strong enough for the task at hand. In addition, overfacing a horse—demanding levels of performance beyond its current training and development—also invites conflict behaviors.

8 Out-of-context expressions of conflict

The effects of chronic stress can spread into the other parts of the horse's life, away from the source of the original conflict. This is true for all animals, including humans. Conflicts and confusion in horse-human interactions tend to raise fear and insecurity levels of horses in human company.

Thus, horses that "fence walk" (pace up and down their paddock boundary) are displaying their lack of clear signal-response uniformities. It is true that horses that are "herd bound" or show separation anxiety—constantly whinnying for equine company, or attempting to stall when leaving other horses—are acting instinctively; it is also true that confused horses become increasingly insecure. As a result, the horse begins desperately to seek equine company.

All problems that occur in the trailer have a direct correlation with failures in leading response qualities. Problems in the race stalls have a direct correlation with leading and riding responses (as well as go and stop). Horses that paw the ground are in conflict about their trained responses (particularly stop) in hand and/or under saddle. These qualities

Left *Pawing is a sign of a confused stop response where the horse has no self-maintained immobility. Kicking out is largely a sign of conflict with the go signal/response.*

need to be retrained and, in some cases, have their context altered.

Training factors have largely been overlooked in connection with stereotypies: Traditional research has tended to concentrate on the altered diet of the animal, its loss of freedom to exercise, and to graze for extended periods. However, confinement and restrictions in grazing result in behavioral conflicts, so it is entirely likely that other conflicts may contribute to these behaviors, particularly those connected with unresolved training conflicts. I have found that many disorders strongly correlate with inconsistencies in responses; horses that exhibit crib biting and weaving, for example, typically have problems with in-hand and under-saddle responses at the Basic attempt and timing levels. In my experience, all of the following can be alleviated through retraining:

- weaving
- windsucking/crib biting
- kicking in stalls
- head shaking
- physiological problems
- hard to catch
- separation anxiety

Training to resolve conflict

The program for resolving conflict behaviors consists of a number of discrete stages, each of which has a clearly defined aim, as follows:

- Reduce trained behaviors to discrete signal-response relationships (in hand: "go," "stop," head down, turn hindlegs; under saddle: "go," "stop," turn forelegs, turn hindlegs).
- Identify the single components of these responses so that they can be retrained (basic attempt, timing, speed and rhythm, line and straightness, connection and outline, adjustability, and proof).
- Identify links between problem behaviors and qualities of trained responses. For example, bucking horses almost always have problems in their "go" response, plus heavy "stop" responses; horses that pull back when tethered have problems with in-hand "go" responses.
- Reinstall (retrain) those responses and light signals via negative reinforcement.
- Apply learning theory and the principles of psychology to the retraining of these qualities.

Contemporary retraining

There are many excellent trainers who have "feel" and instinctively know to pressure and release, particularly under saddle. Many others, however, do not. In general the primacy of stop and go signals in the horse's training is not understood in terms of its relationship to behavior problems: It is not widely realized, for example, that almost every behavior problem involves the horse slowing, quickening, or not responding. Horse trainers frequently issue too many signals at once, such as using whip, spur, and tongue-clucking for "go": Dressage trainers are particularly guilty in this respect. This has largely come about because training evolved before psychology and few trainers (except perhaps the French master Baucher) ever questioned the impossibility of the horse reponding simultaneously to two opposing signals.

Conflicts are common when the same or similar signals are used to elicit different responses. In dressage, the reins are sometimes used not only to stop or slow the horse, but also *without any slowing* to "put the horse on the bit." Some horses habituate to the signals and become dull; others express an escalating series of hyperreactive responses and chronic conflict behaviors. Because contemporary training is largely unsystematic, many trainers believe that "roundness" is the vital first step. So before the rider has any uniform responses from the horse's legs—before establishing speed, rhythm, or straightness—the head carriage is forced. This subjects the horse to even more conflict.

Implying subjective mental states in horses leads to a variety of training approaches. At one end of the scale, punishment is doled out without any sense of immediate contingency upon behavior. Punishment itself can never be very effective; it doesn't train a behavior, just tries to extinguish one. Other methods involve simply increasing the intensity of schooling sessions, often within the same flawed learning format that caused the problem in the first place.

In some cases, symptoms rather than causes are targeted. A horse that paws in the trailer might be fitted with a heavy chain around its knee that hurts during pawing, when the cause of this problem is blurred leading responses. Some trainers even believe that hitting the rearing horse over the head with a bag of water or an egg will convince it that it is bleeding and that somehow this will force it to reconsider its actions. Horses that do not stop well are placed in harsher bits, rather than attempting to retrain the "stop" response. This approach takes no account of the *reasons* for the behavior. It does not deal with the "go" problem that caused the training failure. When trainers target symptoms rather than causes, conflict simply reemerges in another context.

A clinical approach to retraining

Horse people generally describe the behavior of their horses in emotional terms, implying subjective mental states or motivations. One of the starting points in retraining is to define behavior in terms of the extent to which it diverges from the correct signal-response entity. Thus "He hates dogs" translates as "a stop problem shows up when the horse sees dogs"; "He just gets excited" (this is conflict-induced hyperreactivity, and no clear signal-response relationships with regard to stop or go); "He is too eager" (a stop problem, and perhaps a go one too); "He is born lazy" (no clear signal-response relationship with go); "He doesn't want to please anymore" (confusion in many responses); and so on.

When trainers reinterpret the problem in terms of retraining go and stop under saddle and in hand, the whole task of retraining becomes much clearer and easier. Some problems, however, require extra training of associated behaviors. For example, headshy horses—apart from the fact that such horses rarely have correct signal-response entities in go and stop in hand—also require some desensitization. The horse has learned that raising its head results in the human hand going away. Thus an important part of

Below It is common practice to make a riding horse submissive by forcing it rounder in its outline (i.e. forcing it to lower its head and arch its neck). A better practice is to train the responses clearly so the horse is relaxed.

retraining is to gradually maintain the contact higher and higher up the horse's head toward its ears, and then finally on its ears. The hand is removed only when the horse does not pull its head away.

Similarly, traveling problems are frequently associated with the trailer itself. For example, when the horse panics or scrambles in the trailer, it is not enough to simply retrain go and stop. It may also be important to block out the window, as scrambling problems are often associated with the view of the scenery swirling by. This can be done with newspaper, and replaced with cross-hatching of electrical tape. The tape is removed piece by piece to remodel the horse's behavior gradually.

Behaviors such as rearing may also require the application of an aversive stimulus while the horse is in the air. (Note that riding a rear is difficult and only professional trainers should attempt to solve such disobediences.) While the problem may be largely solved through go and stop retraining, the horse may

1 Horses learn to be headshy when the act of raising their head results in the removal of the rider's hand.

2 It is therefore important that the rider keeps his hand on the horse's head until it stops moving.

3 The hand can be moved progressively higher and higher on the horse's head when each incremental movement results in calmness.

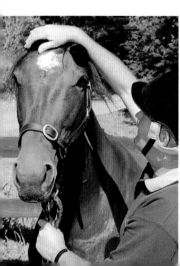

4 The ears are the last to desensitize in the headshy horse. For safety, it is important that the handler keeps his head clear of the horse's head.

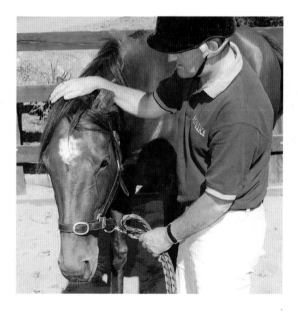

5 Calmness always results when stimulus-response relationships are clearer and hyperreactive states are lost.

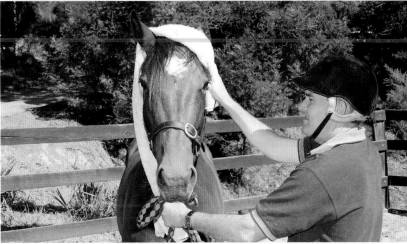

Above *Desensitization of the headshy response can be enhanced or begun with the use of a towel. The towel can be rubbed repeatedly back and forth around the horse's ears and poll.*

learn to trial rearing at every opportunity, regardless of the level of conflict. As the horse's legs leave the ground the rider may perceive that it turns one way or the other (usually to the left). While the horse is on its way up and down the rider tugs the right rein strongly enough to result in the horse turning right a little on landing. This targets the problem and also ensures that rearing is not a favorite practice. The horse should not be pressured while at the highest point in case it loses balance and topples over. The rider must be adept at leaning forward enough so as

not to rely on the reins for balance. A horse that has learned to "flip" over suddenly from a "frozen" halt is dangerous and should not be ridden. Rearing is very dangerous. A horse can lose balance and fall over on the rider. This problem needs to be addressed by a professional for both horse and rider's safety.

Horses that buck have lost a large proportion of the qualities of the go response, and the stop deteriorates as the horse bucks through the rider's attempts to stop it. These must be thoroughly retrained in hand so that the horse can be led in a

1 The horse has reared and spun away from an object—in this case a trash bin.

2 Because the release of the turn rein-pressure rewards the turn response, the rider must maintain the rein if it is safe to do so. The rider looks in the direction of his proposed line.

3 The rider leans forward as in jumping. At the highest point of the rear the reins are softened so that the horse doesn't lose balance. On the way down again the turn rein-pressure is continued to retake the line.

straight line at trot and then abruptly halted so that it skids from the rein pressure, and its hindlegs "freeze." A few repetitions of such clear stop responses help ensure that under saddle the horse can be immobilized the instant it trials a buck. Under saddle go and stop should be clearly retrained.

Most behavior problems involving tension and losses of line and straightness, connection, and outline involve transitions, with variations in pressure of either go or stop. These can be retrained using full transitions or half-halts; the rider emphasizes the rein aspect of the half-halt for quickening, leaning, and outline problems, and the leg signals for go or slowing problems.

If horse trainers adhered to basic principles of animal training that arise from learning theory and cognitive science, the amount of wastage in the equine world would be drastically lowered. Riders and trainers could drop mindless training methodologies that they do not understand and that are too complex for the horse to grasp. Instead, trainers would be free to develop their own strategies, based on sound theoretical knowledge of how horses learn their training tasks, and the principles of shaping and reinforcement.

Horses that buck have lost a large proportion of the qualities of the go response, and the stop deteriorates as the horse bucks through the rider's attempts to stop it.

4 When the line is corrected, go forward training is resumed through pressure and release for each correct step. Soon the horse is relaxed beside the obstacle.

Above and left *Before the rider can retrain the go responses in the bucking horse, the stop must also be retrained. This is best done in hand by pressuring an unconditional stop from the reins so that the hindlegs "freeze" and lower. This trains a "skid stop" and should be tested at the trot. Under saddle the rider will then have some control to stop and then retrain the go signal.*

CHAPTER

9 THE FUTURE

OVER THE CENTURIES, THE IMPORTANCE OF THE HORSE IN WAR AND AGRICULTURE PLANTED THE EQUINE FIRMLY IN THE FERTILE GARDENS OF OUR COLLECTIVE IMAGINATIONS, WHERE MYTHS AND LEGENDS ARE BORN AND PROTECTED AGAINST THE MORE RATIONAL FORCES OF THE HUMAN PSYCHE. THE HORSE, BY BIRTHRIGHT A BEAUTIFUL ANIMAL, BECAME EVEN MORE GLORIOUS, ENSHRINED, AND HALLOWED.

But this animal is not just a mythological creature and a metaphor for human frailties; it is a living, breathing animal. And reality is often a frail vehicle for our deepest hopes and dreams. We celebrate the horse but we also abuse it. Starkly, in real life, the notion of the cherished, benevolent horse stands beside the idea of the malevolent one: the bad, mean rogue horse that refuses to please humankind. The proposition of the benevolent horse automatically confronts us with its nemesis. The notion of the malevolent horse is the source of a significant proportion of horse welfare problems today and has been throughout history; it is the dark side of ascribing human mental characteristics to horses.

The disadvantages of this anthropomorphic view are reflected in the high wastage statistics of horses in all disciplines of performance training. Yet, despite this, trainers through the ages have been successful in obtaining desired results. Great trainers work according to some or all of the principles of learning theory, or else their efforts would not be successful. Great trainers have excellent timing and clear, consistent training methods; they just explain them in ways that are at odds with the horse's true mental capabilities.

That is why great trainers are often unable to extrapolate their riding skills to other areas of horse training, such as work in hand. For example, I have seen brilliant riders unable to train horses to load onto trailers effectively. They could not transfer their instinctive talents to other areas of horse training. Because they did not perceive their skills in terms of a theoretical knowledge of behavior principles, they were at a loss to explain them appropriately to others. This lack of a scientific approach is behind the widely held view that great horsemen are "born, not made."

Little training psychology is found in the manuals of what is reputedly the largest youth movement in the Western world—the Pony Club. The same is generally true for the greatest texts on horse training—barely a word on reward–reinforcement or on training principles. No training manuals for animal species are as bereft of training psychology as those of equestrian literature. Yet no other training situation comes with the degree of risk inherent in having an animal with the speed, size, and impulses of the horse working in such close proximity to humans.

The behavioral sciences have been more of a hindrance than a help to trainers. The divergence between ethology (the science of animal behavior) and psychology, and differences within the field of psychology itself, have rendered these disciplines impotent in terms of the assistance provided to horse trainers. Because animal behaviorists have little training in learning theory, they have reinforced misinterpretations of learning theory. While psychology provides us with the theory to describe training, most analyses of negative reinforcement can be found in the dusty archives of mid-twentieth century behaviorism. Yet riders have held reins in their hands for centuries, and used their legs for good reasons of safety and efficiency, methods that still apply to training today. Science should promote ways to understand more about negative reinforcement and in particular how ridden animals such as horses, camels, and elephants learn their signals, and how such learning can be achieved optimally.

Lessons from history

Right In performance sports, the horse must respond obediently to subtleties of rein and leg signals. There is a need for further research into the mechanics of negative reinforcement.

History has much to teach us about training theory. For example French classical training places particular emphasis on self-carriage and maintaining independence of rein and leg signals. The great French master, Baucher, devised a training scale where one quality is trained before another, which concurs with the principle of "shaping" repsonses.

During the last century, the German system of training evolved, based partly on the teachings of the Italian master, Caprilli, the French master de la Guérinière, the traditions of the school of Hanover, and the teachings of the German masters Seegar, Seidler, and Steinbrecht. Integral to this system is the German training scale—also a progressive scale that shapes a uniform outcome. This training scale is one of the reasons why Germany has been at the forefront of international equestrian competition for the last 50 years.

Dressage, showing, and racing

Training has to date been regarded as an art rather than as an exact science; and as an art it has been subject to the whims of fashion. From the point of view of equine welfare, the most disastrous fashion change in dressage and showing in recent times has been the emphasis on a shorter neck and "behind the vertical" outline. The trend in the last few decades has been for many dressage trainers throughout the world, even at the highest levels, to use opposing signals (stop and go) concurrently. Putting the horse "deeper and rounder" through simultaneous go and stop pressures is seen as a way of obtaining "submission" or "respect." Horses that apparently "need" this treatment are simply not fully under stimulus control. With some horses, such training may superficially result in habituation. However with many others, it is the beginning of a downward spiral of conflict behavior.

The judging of dressage and showring horses requires changes that objectively reflect a censure of tension in the competition horse. In dressage, judging already has a reasonably objective base. However there is still a need for further development of judging guidelines in which specific points are deducted for behaviors such as tail-swishing, teeth-grinding, and other conflict behaviors. Self-carriage, that is when the horse travels with a light rein and contact, and has self-maintained rhythm, straightness, and outline is a necessity, not an ideal. It should be a mandatory aspect of training and competition riding in those sports that demand "contact" to test for self-carriage through the release of the reins for a couple of strides at all levels. If the horse is in self-carriage these qualities will not change during this release. Not surprisingly, there is now a call for a re-emphasis on lightness in performance horses.

Correct training is relevant for all horses, not just pleasure and sport horses. In racing, jockeys and track riders frequently use the whip when the horse *cannot* go any faster; they sometimes stop the whip when the horse has *not* gone faster, or they continue to use the whip when the horse has *already* gone faster (offered the correct response)—small wonder that whips can be ineffective for some racehorses. However if whips were used as a light signal for acceleration, and were clearly trained so that the jockey used it only to obtain clear acceleration responses, and removed it immediately when the horse accelerated, then the whip would be effective. Moreover, if race trainers clearly knew the potential of trial-and-error learning in training acceleration, there would be little need for whips except during training with the use of whip-taps to reinforce the leg signals. Maximum acceleration could be trained from the rider's "hands and heels" action.

Racehorses are frequently confused and tense during in-hand work. Sometimes trainers complain that they haven't the time to train in-hand work, yet published research shows that tense horses in saddling enclosures are statistically less likely to win races than calm ones. The downside of current ways of thinking is apparent in the large numbers of tense, poorly trained horses that buck their riders off, travel crookedly, and refuse to enter barrier stalls.

The universality of conflict

The interpretation of problem behaviors as a sign of conflict within the signal–response mechanism does not simply apply to horses. Cognitive scientists describe in general terms the manifestation of various stress responses when signals do not consistently

Left *The tendency over the past few decades has been the shortening of necks and the loss of self-carriage. Yet as far back as the eighteenth century, equestrian literature espoused the importance of self carriage presumably because of its effects on behavior.*

produce uniform responses. This approach applies just as readily to all animals. Captive animals are frequently trained to perform various tasks. For example, many animals such as seals, dolphins, bears, and elephants are frequently trained with secondary positive reinforcers such as clickers or whistles, to present their teeth or limbs for veterinary work and sometimes to enter cages and raceways. It is generally acknowledged that individual animals vary in their "obedience" to their commands. The recalcitrant animals are generally described with anthro-pomorphic explanations such as, "he doesn't want to work today," or "he doesn't feel like cooperating." What the animals are demonstrating, in fact, are diminished signal–response relationships, making them prime candidates for conflict behaviors such as stereotypies (including fence walking, weaving, and swaying, and oral neuroses such as excessive biting, licking, and mauling—themselves, others, or inanimate objects).

This deterioration may occur as a result of food satiation, because the reinforcer in most positive reinforcement schedules is food. The contemporary approach to resolving such issues is to "enrich" the animal's environment. Environmental enrichment is always a positive remedial measure (since the animal's brains have evolved to deal with complex multidimensional landscapes, and much larger home ranges). However conflict behavior requires more than just enrichment. Enrichment does not always lessen conflict behavior. We should remember that, in the wild state, animals have evolved to be able to solve dilemmas through their behavioral responses. In cages and in training this is almost always not necessarily so. When signal–response relationships deteriorate, animals sometimes cease to accept the physical boundaries of their territories or cages. Although animals evolved to cope with the pressures of man the hunter, the pressures applied by man the trainer remain at odds with the evolution of the animals we choose to train.

It is also worth contemplating that the same mechanisms apply to human behavior. Brains have evolved to a standard in the way they work, and so mechanisms that are found in mammals generally apply to humans as well. The major difference is in the size of the prefrontal cortex—the seat of human imagination and abstract thought. This complicates human behavior to the point where humans may develop psychotic behaviors, and project, amplify, and suppress certain emotions and experiences.

Horses are therefore not unique in their tendency to become confused about training signals. What I have tried to demonstrate throughout this book is that training is about ensuring that the horse's legs are under the consistent "stimulus control" of the handler, driver, or rider, and that problems are largely manifest in a random quickening or slowing on the horse's part. While secondary cues such as seat, voice, and position are important, trainers should go beyond them when problems arise, to repair primary responses of leg and rein signals first. Because the rider's hands only have the power to slow one or both forelegs (then ultimately the hindlegs), and the rider's legs have the power to activate one or both hindlegs, correcting behaviors under saddle should also be seen in that mechanistic context. Thus the trainer should identify which legs are quickening or slowing during a behavior problem and correct appropriately.

Trainers will see that there are correlations between all problem behaviors and deficits in rein and leg signal responses, both in hand and under saddle: one or some legs move too fast or too slow. For example, the horse that is heavier on the right rein also doesn't turn right easily. When the rider on that same horse slows its steps to very tiny steps using just the reins, the right front leg takes bigger steps, and the same is seen in hand. Finally, when we look at problems within the context of the scale from basic

attempt to connection and outline, we see that quickening and slowing resistances become increasingly subtle to the point where head tossing is more visible than the associated speed change.

Because of the horse's instinct to run from fear, it also tends to run away from confusion and this is why conflict behavior manifests itself in tension—it is the horse's attempt to flee. When fleeing is thwarted, the body stays at various levels of high alert, which if maintained on a permanent basis results in chronic stress and serious health and welfare problems. Trainers should think carefully about allowing hyperreactive responses to persist on the mistaken assumption that they should just "work through them."

The potential of correct training

On the other side of the coin, the potential for performance horse trainers from racing through to dressage is enormous, if trainers interpreted responses during training interactions as simply that the animal either gives the correct response or it does not. Then, working through the system of progressively shaping the correct response from major incorrect qualities down to minor ones step by step, training all the behaviors to become uniform and to arise from light signals (especially the reins), is essential to avoid conflict behavior. The following ten principles should be adhered to in all horse-training disciplines:

- Primary signal–response relationships should be trained or retrained initially by negative reinforcement, to diminish random mobility responses
- Adhere to the timing of pressure release training, so that signals rapidly shrink to light signals, and return to it when problems strike with a response that is related to that signal
- Train one signal for each response. Back-up pressure can be provided by the whip-tap
- Train one response (e.g., "go") at any one moment
- Progressively shape one quality (e.g., "speed and rhythm") at a time
- Train the horse's legs before the head and neck outline
- Train and maintain self-carriage
- Do not overload the horse with too many repetitions, especially before habits are set

- Use error-free training to delete hyperreactive responses
- Remember the reward up to timing level is the release of pressure; after that, use caressing and associated voice rewards.

As humans we will never know what it is to be a horse. All we can do is use the tools of objective inquiry to determine the exact nature of equine mentality. While it seems clear that the horse does not think in the analytical, insightful human way, we should also be careful not to rule out thought altogether, because of the fuzzy line that separates emotions and thought. The hardest question of all is the one that asks "How does the horse think?" The most important point to acknowledge is that the horse does not think in the way that humans do, and that to impose expectations based on our own mental abilities onto the horse is unjust as well as inaccurate and inefficient.

In many ways this book is more about the truth about humans than it is about horses. It is our responsibility to treat the horse according to its nature, rather than according to our own. It is to be hoped that the horse remains with us forever, but to ensure that, we must be honest with ourselves. If the horse were an animal with the degree of consciousness of a dolphin or a chimpanzee, exploiting it as we do would be ideologically questionable. However because the horse most likely has no insight into its behavior, it is therefore perfectly content to habituate to all the things that we impose on it and to form clear habits. We must learn to be fair and ethical custodians of these animals.

We need to abandon the notion of the benevolent horse, the horse that does things for trust, respect, and love. Real love needs no compensation. To love something or someone requires getting to know them as accurately as possible. That is why mythologies can be so unhelpful—they paint a distorted picture that is more about our insecurities that anything else. The trouble with mythologizing horses is that it shields people from real knowledge and insidiously makes them dependent on others. Knowledge on the other hand is empowering—it provides people with dignity because they are able to understand the processes. For students of horsemanship it allows them to engage in dialogue rather than remain passive recipients of training dogma.

The integration of training psychology and horsemanship has the potential to propel horse training in all disciplines to unimagined heights. In the meantime it drastically lowers the danger that accompanies horse handling and riding. Above all it will free the horse from the confusions of the past and the well-meaning but stubborn mindsets of humanity. This proposition does not necessarily mean that all horses will be easy to train—the influence of genes means that there will always be a variation. However it does mean that all horses will be trainable within their own physical limits, and that those horses that are outside the square of traditional training strategies may now be approached with a different, more appropriate and benign set of tools. When we strip the horse of the misty veil of our dreams, it emerges, even more remarkable than ever.

GLOSSARY

Aids *Signals or cues by which the rider gives instructions to the horse.* Natural aids *include the rider's hands, legs, body, and voice.*

Balk *To stall or refuse to move forward, or toward something.*

Canter *Three-beated gait, called the lope in Western riding, in which one hindleg strides first (the leading leg), followed by the opposite diagonal pair, and finally the opposite foreleg.*

Connection *The light and neutral contact that exists between the rider's hands and the horse's mouth, and between the rider's legs and the horse's sides.*

Crib-biting *or* **Cribbing** *A stable vice in which the horse hooks his teeth onto something solid, such as the door of his stable, and sucks air through his open mouth.* Windsucking *is similar but doesn't involve contact with the teeth.*

Croup *The highest point on the horse's rump.*

Dressage *The art of training horses to perform movements in a balanced, supple, obedient, and enthusiastic manner.*

Farrier *Skilled craftsperson who shoes horses, also known as a blacksmith.*

Flexion *The yielding of the horse's lower jaw to the pressure of the bit, with the neck held high and arched, and bent at the poll.*

Gait *The various types of forward motion of the horse, including walk, trot, canter, and gallop.*

Gallop *Four-beated gait, in which each foot touches the ground separately.*

Half-halt *A brief, almost simultaneous application of opposing go and stop signals, used to collect and engage the horse's hindquarters.*

Halter *or* **Headcollar** *A headpiece with lead rope attached, used for leading a horse when it is not wearing a bridle, or for tying up in a stable.*

Hard-wired behaviors *Instinctive behaviors that are present in a horse at birth.*

Headshy *A horse is headshy if it withdraws its head in fear when a handler attempts to touch its head.*

In-hand *An animal being led or controlled from the ground, rather than driven or ridden.*

Inside leg *The leg or legs of rider or horse on the inside of any circle or track being described.*

Leading leg *The front leg; the leg that appears to be leading the sequence at a canter or gallop.*

Line and straightness *The horse's self-maintenance of direction ("line") and the consequent "straightness" throughout the horse's body length that follows when the horse does not drift one way or another, but moves in the direction signaled by the rider.*

Lunge *The act of training a horse by working it in various paces in a circle while it is on a long "lunge" rein.*

Outline *The shape made by the horse, from the head and neck, along the back, and around the hindquarters to the hocks.*

Oxer *A strong fence consisting of railings. It can be an ascending oxer, with the front rail lower than the back rail, or a square oxer (also known as a parallel), with front and back rails of the same height.*

Poll *The bony apex of the horse's head, between the ears.*

Primary signals *Signals used to elicit basic responses: The legs, leg, reins, and rein signals elicit go, yield, stop, and turn responses respectively.*

Quarter horse *A breed of horse bred for sprinting over short distances, and commonly used in Western and pleasure riding.*

Stereotypies *Neurotic, repetitive behaviors that are thought to be mechanisms for coping with stress.*

Stimulus control *When a behavior is under stimulus control, it can be elicited by the trainer using a discrete signal.*

Thoroughbred *A breed of horse selectively bred for racing.*

Transition *The act of changing from one gait to another. Walk to trot and trot to canter are known as* upward transitions. *Canter to trot and trot to walk are known as* downward transitions.

Trot *Moderate-speed gait in which the horse moves from one diagonal pair of legs to the other, with a period of suspension in between.*

Wastage *The proportion of working animals put down for health, behavioral, or other reasons when the animal is no longer deemed suitable for its original intended use.*

Wither *Point at the bottom of the neck of a horse from which the height is measured.*